Metacognition and Study Skills

Pupils often make poor choices when it comes to independent learning because they don't intuitively understand how to learn. In the classroom too, they typically misjudge how well they understand new concepts, overestimate the accuracy of their own examples, and underestimate how much they forget. This book reveals how a metacognitive approach to teaching can help overcome these challenges and support pupils in their learning. This approach can help them in developing the skills to become successful, self-regulated learners.

Drawing on key research from cognitive science, this book explores how metacognition works in practice and argues that it is a complex skill best developed over months and years at school. It provides a blueprint for 'learning to learn' alongside 'quick wins' that teachers can implement straight away. Chapters cover:

- The metacognitive processes that underpin effective learning
- Myths about learning, and how pupils' memory really works
- Quick-to-apply classroom strategies for before, during, and after tasks
- Different independent study techniques and how to embed them
- Developing a culture of metacognition

Full of practical strategies and case studies, this is essential reading for all teachers who want to help their pupils become successful learners in school as well as independent learners for their exam revision and beyond.

Jonathan Firth is a teacher, author, and researcher. Having taught psychology at secondary school level for many years, he now works at the University of Strathclyde, Glasgow, leading lectures and seminars on undergraduate and postgraduate courses, carrying out research, and supervising students.

Metacognition and Study Skills

A Guide for Teachers

Jonathan Firth

Routledge
Taylor & Francis Group

LONDON AND NEW YORK

Designed cover image: © Getty Images

First published 2025
by Routledge
4 Park Square, Milton Park, Abingdon, Oxon OX14 4RN

and by Routledge
605 Third Avenue, New York, NY 10158

Routledge is an imprint of the Taylor & Francis Group, an informa business

British Library Cataloguing-in-Publication Data
A catalogue record for this book is available from the British Library

ISBN: 978-1-032-48016-9 (hbk)
ISBN: 978-1-032-48015-2 (pbk)
ISBN: 978-1-003-38697-1 (ebk)

DOI: 10.4324/9781003386971

Typeset in Galliard
by SPi Technologies India Pvt Ltd (Straive)

Contents

About the Author

Dr Jonathan Firth is a teacher, author, and researcher. Having taught psychology at secondary school level for many years, he now works at the University of Strathclyde, Glasgow, leading lectures and seminars on undergraduate and postgraduate courses, carrying out research, and supervising students.

Jonathan's research interests focus on the applications of psychology to education, in particular memory, metacognition, and creativity. He sends a regular newsletter about memory and metacognition for educators; details can be found at jonathanfirth.co.uk. He lives on the west coast of Scotland.

Acknowledgements

I would like to thank my brilliant wife Fiona for her support throughout this project. Her contribution to this book and previous ones cannot be overstated. I'd also like to acknowledge the encouragement and patience of my children, Alex and Duncan – always fun company and happy to indulge my questioning about their study habits! In terms of my thinking on metacognition, I must recognise the many colleagues, students, and contacts throughout the education system – people too numerous to name but who have developed my understanding in a multitude of ways. I would like to gratefully acknowledge the many researchers cited within, on whose work and ideas the entire book depends. Finally, I'd like to thank my parents for a lifetime of support and kindness.

Introduction

This book is about metacognition – what it is, how it works, and how to support it among your students. By reading and engaging with the various chapters, you will develop a comprehensive understanding of why metacognition is so important. It will help you to feel informed and empowered to make changes to your teaching and your wider practice.

Metacognition means thinking about thinking and includes a broad range of things, such as

- A young child's capacity to choose strategies and 'course-correct' during learning;
- An older student's ability to plan their work and to reflect on later feedback;
- How a teacher thinks about their students' progress or about learning in general.

It should be stated right away that engaging with metacognition is no magic bullet that will somehow solve all of your classroom problems. That is no more the case for metacognition than it is for any other aspect of evidence-based pedagogy. Learning is complex, and there are many barriers to our students' success, attainment, and wellbeing. In addition, even useful techniques are not always fully understood or embraced by students, limiting their impact.

However, the reason that metacognition has become such a hot topic in education is that researchers have come to realise how central it is to learning. Metacognitive processes are happening every day in every lesson. What's more, learners who think strategically are more successful, meaning that a metacognitive approach can significantly boost attainment. Don't just take my word for it, though – the evidence is explored in Chapter 1.

As well as being widespread, metacognition has certain other important features that make it valuable for practice. It is to some extent developmental, in that children get better at it over time, but learners of any age can engage with metacognitive strategies. This implies a very practical approach, and one that does not imply a focus on ability. Metacognitive strategies are all about improvement. Anyone, at any stage in their learning, can think more (or think more *accurately*) about their learning.

What's more, compared to the slow progress that characterises the learning of basic skills and knowledge, improving a student's metacognition can be transformative over

DOI: 10.4324/9781003386971-1

1

short timescales. Strategies can be applied to multiple tasks or situations. We can see a radical change in how an individual plans and structures their work, for example, or an overnight change in the study strategies they choose to use, even if these changes will still take time to practise and take root.

Metacognition and Professionalism

As the earlier examples suggest, it's not just students who engage in metacognition. We can also consider its role among educators. Our own beliefs about learning are not automatically accurate; a deeper and more evidence-based understanding of how learning works will help with making good decisions in the classroom.

My own exploration of the topic has led to a certain humility. Cognitive science, like any other scientific endeavour, has a tentative element. We are dealing with a subject matter which repeatedly warns that even experts can't always trust their own judgement due to issues such as the curse of knowledge (biases caused by expertise) or the failure of skills learned in one domain to transfer to another. Having some experience in the science of learning doesn't mean that understanding or applying every new idea will be straightforward.

All the same, this awareness of the complexities involved in learning can sound a useful note of caution when one is faced with new ideas and policies. More positively, a metacognitive understanding of how learning works can help guide our choices from lesson planning to feedback.

New and Fashionable?

Some teachers are (rightly) suspicious when they hear about the latest idea in education. So, how do we know that metacognition isn't another fad or myth, something that is promoted today but will be in the recycle bin in a year or two?

There certainly are plenty of people who advocate for educational changes or different approaches. However, such claims are not all equal. From people who write about education in newspapers to celebrities weighing in with their opinions on what teachers are doing wrong, many supposedly radical ideas are based in little more than hearsay, personal experience, and opinion. And talking about problems is not as valuable as coming up with a clear plan for solving them.

Metacognition is different. It is based on a thorough and extensive body of research, itself connected to fundamentals of memory and other areas of cognitive science (as we will see in Chapter 2). And while I will sometimes identify problems in this book, the focus will be on sharing highly specific and evidence-informed solutions.

Granted, we can't assume that everything that has been labelled 'metacognition' is necessarily going to be helpful. Programmes and strategies vary, and not everyone who talks about metacognition actually understands it. As practitioners, we must be able to distinguish between evidence-based claims and over-simplistic mantras. We should proceed with caution – and with knowledge. This is what we mean by education being evidence-based.

This book, therefore, aims to provide a more thoughtful, sound, and well-worked-out look at challenges facing educators and their students and the potential of a metacognitive approach to teaching as part of the solution. If you've had the misfortune of attending continuing professional development (CPD) or in-service sessions promoting educational myths, I think you'll find this book very different indeed!

Origins of the Concept

While I certainly don't think that metacognition is the latest fad, it's true that psychologists developed the term quite late in relative terms. As a research area, it began to gain attention in the 1970s, when John Flavell noted that memory depends upon an active monitoring process that he called "a kind of meta-memory" (Flavell, 1971, p. 277). The research really gathered pace in the 1980s, with further important theories established in the early 1990s. Compared to some areas of psychology research, that's all quite recent.

However, the relative youth of the research tradition doesn't change the fact that effective learners have been engaging in metacognition for centuries, even if nobody used that specific term. The Ancient Greeks exhorted each of us to "know thyself", and devised mnemonics to tackle forgetting. Freud, a psychologist who focused on unconscious mental processes, felt that achieving insight into our own thoughts was essential. Nowadays, metacognition is seen as a key strand of the science of learning (e.g. Newcomb, 2023), but the processes involved (planning, strategies, etc.) have been around for a long time.

In short, metacognition is and has always been everywhere, but it was not a focus of cognition research, teacher professionalism, or educational practice until more recently. Likewise, most students have never heard of it and are unlikely to be thinking about their own learning in a strategic way.

This brings us to the point where the profession as a whole can benefit from a deep, systematic, and evidence-based understanding of metacognition. This book journeys into the metacognition research, exploring how it works in practice and outlining dozens of ways to apply it in the classroom.

Using This Book

The structure of this book is as follows: first, we will explore some of the fundamentals of metacognition, its processes and purpose, building on what has been said in this introduction so far. We will then look at its connections to memory principles. In doing so, I aim to show how memory is built on shifting sands, with our memories and our understanding of these memories (as both students and teachers) very open to errors and misconceptions. If you are already an expert on issues such as theories of memory, schemas, the unreliability of memory, or the performance vs. learning distinction, you can skip Chapter 2.

Next, we will look at 'quick wins' – the things that I would recommend any teacher to start doing straight away (Chapter 3) – and, over the subsequent three chapters, explore task-relevant aspects of metacognition that can be applied before, during, and after a task takes place.

The later chapters of the book look at implications for literacy, at self-regulated learning and study skills, and at developing and supporting an ethos of metacognitive learning in your classroom. Finally, I propose a 'metacognition manifesto' for your school/college as a whole and for engaging with the concept in a more system-wide manner.

As you work through the book, there as a case study in every chapter. These focus on a range of curriculum areas and student ages. Even if the context in a particular case study doesn't match what you teach, hopefully you will see that these are just practical illustrations of the concepts covered.

There are also several tasks throughout the book. These often guide your implementation of new ideas, though some are more reflective, prompting you to think about when and how metacognitive processes will be relevant to your context.

Finally, each chapter ends with a summary and some discussion questions. The discussion questions are aimed at supporting CPD groups of various kinds. If you meet to discuss this book, or just one of the chapters from it, these questions can act as prompts. And if you are engaging with the book in this way, please do reach out to me – I always love to hear from practitioners who are as passionate about metacognition as I am.

I very much hope you enjoy this book and get as much inspiration from reading it as I did from engaging with the ideas that went into it.

The Logic of Focusing on How to Learn

What is metacognition, anyway? This is a question I am asked a lot! Many people are curious or recognise the concept's importance. Fewer could confidently define it. And for newer or student teachers, it may just be an alarmingly long bit of terminology to remember!

When explaining metacognition to other teachers (or student teachers), I find that the easiest way to understand it is to think first about what *cognition* is. And then anything that involves thinking about that cognition can be defined as metacognition.

To make that a bit more concrete, here are some of the main cognitive processes that researchers tend to focus on and study:

- Attention;
- Memory;
- Knowledge and beliefs;
- Thinking, reasoning, and understanding;
- Perception of sensory information.

All of these are in themselves complex processes, but they are also unavoidable, every-day processes. They are things that students engage in every single day when they are studying and learning. It's impossible to write an essay, for example, without focusing attention, drawing on your memory, using language skills, and so on.

Most or all of the cognitive processes above will be covered in any Introduction to Psychology course, and each will warrant its own chapter in the supporting textbook. Indeed, the application of every one of those cognitive processes could be the focus of a book in its own right, and each is explored in dozens of new scientific papers every year.

We will consider only on the part of that research which illuminates metacognition and which is particularly relevant to the classroom. And for now, it's enough for you to draw on your existing understanding of each of the processes above. Memory involves taking in new ideas and retaining them, for example, and beliefs concern what we think about the world or ourselves.

DOI: 10.4324/9781003386971-2

The Meta Level

Now that the role of cognition has been highlighted, what is metacognition? Consider the following sentence (source: Nelson, 1996, p. 105):

Thiss sentence contains threee errors.

It's a simple example, but it gives us a nice idea of what it means to consider something on a 'meta' level. In the sentence, there are two errors of spelling and one error that is more *about* the sentence itself. Hopefully, it's easy to see that one category of error is about the thing – the object – and the other category involves reflecting on that object on a more abstract level.

This is very similar to how psychologists view the connection between cognition and metacognition. Cognition includes everyday classroom mental processes – memory, thinking, and so forth – that are involved in carrying out a learning task. Metacognition involves reflecting on these processes from a higher level. They are processes that are 'about' the more basic cognition. This might include the following:

- Thinking about thinking;
- Beliefs that we have about how memory works;
- Paying attention to our own language use.

In short, metacognition could involve any one of the processes mentioned earlier reflecting on itself or on another cognitive process.

As a practical example, remembering a vocabulary item is cognition. Thinking about how or why you remembered or forgot an item is metacognition. So is understanding of why you remembered the word or your anticipation of forgetting in the future. Your knowledge of strategies to better remember new vocabulary in future also forms part of metacognition.

Hopefully, you can see that each of these examples involves cognition about the process, rather than carrying out the process itself.

Task 1.1

The bullet points above illustrate three examples of how two cognitive processes could be linked together to become metacognitive processes. Try to think of a few more examples of your own and note them down.

In future, if you're ever wondering whether something 'counts' as metacognition or not, you could stop and apply this approach. Consider whether the example is a cognitive process that reflects on another cognitive process. If not, it probably shouldn't be seen as a form of metacognition.

By the way, for this and other tasks in this book, it will be good to have a notebook handy. Referring back to it will help you to enhance your practice over the long term.

With that established, I want to explore the role of metacognition in teaching in this chapter and expand on what was said in the Introduction to this book. More: I want to present the rationale for a metacognitive approach to teaching. Although we *could* focus just on the cognitive level (memory, attention, etc.), there are good reasons to think that ignoring metacognition is a mistake.

Metacognition can be seen in terms of oversight of the learning process, a kind of control panel or governance system. It is the part of the mind that focuses on what we are doing and why. Included in this are the essential strategies that play a role in learning, from very specific techniques (such as how to do long division) to more general ideas about how to learn, how to consolidate, how to focus, how to stop yourself from forgetting, and so forth.

Particularly in the latter case (general ideas about how to learn), there is good evidence that students don't readily pick these ideas up by themselves, and they are generally not taught them either. Psychological literacy in how the mind works cannot be taken for granted (Firth, 2022). Students may face a lifetime of underachievement if they don't attain this understanding. At the very least, their learning will be slower and more haphazard than necessary.

Research evidence suggests that even more high-attaining students – those on track to go to university or already studying there – maintain flawed, inefficient approaches to learning (e.g. Bjork & Bjork, 2023; Dirkx et al., 2019). As explained in the next chapter (see Chapter 2), many will misunderstand learning, forget a lot, and fail to realise when their memories have been distorted.

You may still harbour some doubt that a metacognitive approach to teaching is the solution to this problem. Couldn't it just be the case that learning is hard, that students will never fully understand how their minds work? Arguably, many will muddle through somehow. And teachers and students have managed for centuries, prior to the research into metacognition taking off.

However, although teachers and students certainly have been getting by for years, this doesn't necessarily mean that they haven't been engaging in metacognitive practices. It could be the case that the most successful teachers were in fact engaging in metacognitive practices and developing them among their students, even if they didn't use that term. It's also possible that for many of the more successful students, the learning journey was a lot harder than it needed to be! Wouldn't *you* have liked a set of instructions on how to learn, rather than having to figure it out for yourself?

Later in this chapter, we will explore some of the research evidence around the direct impact that metacognition can have, including on students' self-regulated study. But before we do, it's time to delve a little deeper into the idea of the metacognitive level, in order to see more clearly how metacognitive processes can be influenced by the teacher.

Different Levels of Thinking

There has been a lot of research on metacognition over the past few decades, but perhaps the clearest explanation of its role was presented in a model created by Nelson and Narens (1990). Their model shows mental processes split into two main levels:

- Cognition
- Metacognition

The metacognitive level can be seen as a reflection of the cognitive level and also as a control system. Most of our everyday thinking and learning, and that of our students, is happening at the cognitive level. But whenever a learner thinks about their own thinking or learning, this is represented in the metacognitive level. You can see it as a very imperfect mirror image of the cognitive level.

The metacognitive level also provides guidance to the cognitive level, and so the whole system operates as a feedback loop. The metacognitive level both mirrors cognition and also sends guidance and instructions via 'control processes' to help us learn (Figure 1.1).

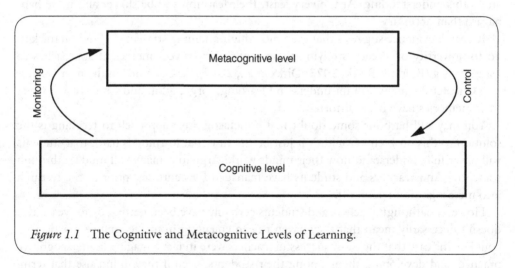

Figure 1.1 The Cognitive and Metacognitive Levels of Learning.

A metacognitive approach to teaching can influence any aspect of this model. We can try to help students to focus more on their learning, thus boosting their 'metacognitive monitoring'. We can try to address the accuracy of the metacognitive level itself in various ways, thus improving their 'metacognitive knowledge' and the way they think about their own learning. Or we can guide them to draw on the metacognitive level more often or more successfully, targeting its control processes which help students make decisions about how to learn.

Consider the following metacognitive questions that we might ask students in order to prompt metacognition:

- *"Are you on the right track?"*

  This question asks the learner to focus on their current progress, thus boosting their monitoring. Similarly, any time that we ask learners to stop, put their pens down, and think about what they have just done, we are giving them a nudge to monitor more.

- *"What order should you do these tasks in?"*

  This question prompts learners to access their metacognitive knowledge. They will (usually) already possess relevant knowledge about the steps needed to fulfil a familiar task, such as when a Biology student describes the stages of an experiment. When asked to access this knowledge, some may realise that they are uncertain about the details.

- *"Did you do that task correctly?"*

  This question prompts learners to focus on their performance and to check for errors. It causes a control process to kick in – they are accessing their knowledge but also comparing this to what's in their notebooks. This can be relevant when students check spelling, review a graph that they have drawn, or read over their working for a mathematical problem.

These examples are just three of the hundreds of possible metacognitive questions that a teacher (or a student themselves) could ask. There are, accordingly, hundreds of things that we can do or say to affect any of these fundamental processes – monitoring, knowledge, and control. And remember, all of this is in addition to anything that we do to boost the *cognitive* level – improving the learner's basic knowledge and skills, for example – which can in turn be guided by a teacher's metacognitive knowledge of how learning works.

Hopefully, these examples serve to show that there is a lot that a metacognitive approach can do to boost learners' attainment, over and above the other fundamentals of good teaching.

An Absence of Metacognition

We can further clarify what is meant by a metacognitive approach to teaching by considering what the learning setting would look like if this *weren't* happening. What would the absence of metacognitive teaching and learning look like?

In fact, this is not hard to imagine, because it can be observed in almost every school around the world.

A lack of metacognitive practice is happening when schools don't train their students in how to learn, or prompt them to think about what they are doing with new information, and why. It is happening when teachers don't allocate time to a discussion of learning in the classroom, use accurate terminology, or foster a can-do attitude to improvement of skills and strategies. And it is happening when the focus is on the taking in of content, with little or no discussion of what to do with that content.

The previous comment above might seem ironic given that I have emphasised the importance of memory (and will do so again in Chapter 2). However, applying memory in education is not (or *shouldn't* be) about meaningless memorisation (e.g. Firth, 2018). A much better use of memory is to help students retain things so that they can use them flexibly in the future, in their lives and careers.

A metacognitive approach to teaching therefore pushes back against excessive content focus and 'dumb' uses of memory strategies. The focus is not just on the content itself but on what it is useful for. If students are thinking not just about what they 'need to know' but about why they need to know it or what it might be useful for in future, this is already moving into metacognitive territory. They are thinking about the knowledge and about its purpose.

Everyday Metacognition

As has already been mentioned, metacognitive processes are already happening in classrooms. Even if we don't teach metacognition at all, some learners will still pick up on and engage in strategies such as planning and reflection, and there will be evidence of spontaneous classroom thinking that we can consider to be metacognitive. A student may say "I'm stuck" or "This is hard" – these are metacognitive statements! They may also think about whether they are coping with a task, whether their experiment is working, or what their chances of passing an upcoming test are. Again, such thinking is inherently metacognitive.

However, tasks such as writing, as explained in Case Study 1, which are characterised by a lot of intuitive and implicit metacognition, show us that even these spontaneous metacognitive processes are not enough. Such spontaneous metacognition is often insufficiently long-term and strategic, and learners who are not trained in metacognition will not intuitively appreciate matters such as how to tackle their problems instead focusing on details of performance. Without guidance, they are also likely to harbour metacognitive illusions, such as having misconceptions about what a skilled piece of student work looks like or incorrectly assuming that success is a matter of ability rather than skill (see Chapters 2 and 6 for further examples of metacognitive errors).

Case Study 1: A Biology Essay

Kira has written a lot of essays in her time at school, but today she is struggling. It's evening, and the deadline for her Biology essay is midnight. As stress begins to rise, she abandons her original plan, arguing to herself that there is no longer time to work through it systematically.

In the essay, Kira is explaining how Darwin's theory of evolution by natural selection can help us to understand the behaviour of modern mammals. It's an interesting topic, and one that Kira coped well with in class, but as she tries to think of examples and apply the theory, she finds herself getting stuck again and again. She repeatedly rephrases particular sentences to make them clearer and then returns to bits that she has written before, deleting parts that don't sound good.

Kira knows that she should be better at this, but up against a deadline, she can't help but feel that her essay is worthless and that she's going to fail.

Comment on Case Study 1

Case Study 1 will sound familiar to many of us who have worked close to deadlines during our student days or have family members who do so. It also shows that even when students are engaging in everyday metacognition, it may be limited and ineffective.

The case study shows a typical example of the interplay between cognitive and metacognitive levels in real learning situations. Composing a written piece is complex, and it's effortful to retrieve stored knowledge and to come up with spontaneous examples to illustrate a point. We see here that the task is deeply challenging, especially when done under pressure.

Although Kira is certainly thinking about her own thinking and performance – she is being metacognitive – she isn't zooming out and considering broader strategy. She is focusing so much on specific passages and sentences of her essay that very little attention is being paid to more strategic aspects such as her original plan, the overall flow of the piece, or the audience. She may well be judging her work too negatively – her example might not be viewed so harshly by a reader. Kira's attention is also distracted by other factors, especially her deadline.

Therefore, just being metacognitive is not enough. The fact that a student will spontaneously engage in some metacognitive thought as they craft a piece of writing won't always guarantee a good outcome. They may be too focused on the minutiae of a task to consider the bigger picture, fail to notice when they are going astray by veering off track in terms of the original aim of the task, or misjudge the quality of their work. As Graham and Harris (2016, p. 261) explain, "While it is comforting to think that students will learn all they need to know by writing frequently for real purposes, this is simply not the case."

For the teacher, then, practice alone is not enough. It's not sufficient that students spend lots of hours working on relevant tasks (and, indeed, we see in Case Study 1 that Kira has already had a lot of practice of writing essays). These points may put you in mind of the different levels discussed earlier in the chapter. Too much focus on the cognitive level of the task could mean neglecting the metacognitive level.

When there is a focus on metacognition, with selection among a range of possible strategies when completing a task, it needs to be well guided. Students don't just need to think more, but they need accurate self-knowledge (Pintrich, 2002), which won't appear automatically. A metacognitive approach aims to tackle these problems. It aims to build on the low-level, spontaneous metacognition that our students already engage in, and introduce them to a more systematic, evidence-based approach. Students like Kira rely on well-informed teachers to inform and guide them about the best strategies to use.

Contrasts between Approaches

The points above help to highlight key differences between a metacognitive approach to teaching and what I will (for simplicity) call a 'traditional' approach. The traditional approach is influenced by older pedagogies and theories (such as behaviourism and the early days of cognitivism) in that it emphasises repetition and memory and neglects the value of strategy and reflection on learning.

However, it is not just happening in classrooms that feature heavily didactic approaches or that people might decry as 'old-fashioned'. Many classrooms that look very modern and whose teachers appear dynamic and forward-looking take an approach to learning that focuses on short-term repetition of content, unaware of the potential of a metacognitive approach to teaching.

Some of the key contrasts that characterise these two approaches to teaching are summarised in Table 1.1.

As can be seen, there are many differences. Although what I have labelled as a traditional approach comprises a mixture of educational strategies, they all have something important in common: they neglect that metacognitive level. They also fail to harmonise with key principles of human memory; these are explored in Chapter 2.

Some readers might wonder if I have set up a straw-man opponent in my presentation of a traditional approach to teaching. In fact, I don't think the examples on the left of Table 1.1 reflect bad or incompetent teaching. I have worked with many teachers who have taken this approach and who were accomplished practitioners and well liked by their students. The students mostly passed their exams, too. But if our purpose is to develop lifelong learners, then such practitioners are clearly missing a trick. What is the point in studying new material if you can't retain it and/or if you can't use it in new, unpredictable situations? Such an approach might help you to pass a test, but it doesn't do much for your intellect.

Table 1.1 Contrasts between traditional and metacognitive approaches to teaching.

A Traditional Approach	A Metacognitive Approach
An emphasis on repetition	An emphasis on strategy
Assuming that students will hit on appropriate strategies and techniques spontaneously	Directly teaching the best strategies
Focusing on ability	Focusing on skill
A narrative of 'you need to find what works for you'	A narrative that emphasises finding the best, evidence-based techniques
An emphasis on consolidating topic content.	An emphasis on using and transferring topic content flexibly.
An emphasis on covering content in discrete chunks, by topic.	An emphasis on seeing broad links.
Ask 'what' questions.	Ask 'why' questions.
Assumes that learning is permanent once a topic is complete.	Assumes that new ideas and information will be rapidly forgotten unless action is taken.

On the right-hand side of Table 1.1, the emphasis on direct teaching of strategies comes to the fore. As metacognition is largely unseen, it's easy for educators to assume that the necessary internal dialogue and reflection will develop by itself (Bransford et al., 2000). This is an example of the curse of knowledge – the finding that people with high levels of knowledge and skill tend to underestimate the difficulty of these for other people. As we teachers can engage in metacognition ourselves, we assume that it is straightforward for students too. Evidence suggests that this is not the case. A key aspect of the approach is making this more overt, modelling it and discussing it with students along the way.

An emphasis on repetition rather than strategy is another very clear-cut example of how the metacognitive approach differs from common practice. I have heard many teaching colleagues say to me things like, "We don't have time to focus on metacognition, because we are too busy covering the content. There's so much of it!" I feel that this is rather like a builder saying that they are too busy laying bricks to consult the architectural plans. We do sometimes need to step back and consider our purpose.

Research into the Effect of Metacognition

In this chapter so far, we have explored the idea of the metacognitive level and considered what a metacognitive approach to teaching would look like. Let's now survey the research into how metacognition has been applied and consider the impact on students that has been found.

Task 1.2

Consider your expectations in terms of supporting research evidence on metacognition. What would you consider to be convincing evidence? And how big an effect on attainment would you expect metacognition to have, in comparison with other variables such as a teacher's knowledge and skill? Note these things down before you read on!

To preface the research findings, it can be helpful to bear in mind that metacognition is not just one thing. It contains multiple strategies and can be applied to different skills and curriculum areas. It is also important to consider that metacognition is complex to measure and depends in part how we choose to operationalise it for a particular research study. Even if researchers have a clear idea of what they are looking for, they may rely on things like self-report ("Did you use strategy X?") or evidence in the form of artifacts (e.g. students' planning documents) to gauge which strategies (if any) they used.

A lot of the research has focused on particular metacognitive *strategies* connected to how curriculum content is approached. These include goal setting, planning, self-monitoring, self-control, and self-evaluation (e.g. Boekaerts, 1996). However, it's worth bearing in mind that the use of these specific strategies is only part of metacognition and that by focusing on these things specifically (and, sometimes, not all of them), research may be underestimating the benefits of a broader metacognitive approach (Dent & Koenka, 2016).

Evidence of a Significant and Positive Impact of Metacognition

Despite the challenges to this line of research, there is, in general terms, an extensive range of evidence that suggests a significant and positive impact of metacognition on attainment across a range of curriculum areas (Muijs & Bokhove, 2020). Dent and Koenka (2016) found that both metacognitive strategies and cognitive strategies (i.e. things linked more to the cognitive level in the model described in the previous section) correlated with attainment and that, out of the two, metacognitive strategies showed a stronger association. They also argued that this likely underestimated the true impact of metacognitive strategies due to the reliance of student self-report, with studies that measured strategy use at the time of use showing bigger effects.

Another finding arising from the review by Dent and Koenka (2016) is that some aspects of metacognition appear to have more impact than others. Students' use of planning, self-checking, and adjusting seem to be more impactful than goal setting. This could be because students are quite poor at goal setting, though it's also possible that schools are quite good at setting goals for students when they don't do so for themselves.

Research into Metacognition Training

So far, the findings mentioned have focused on studies that look at students' current engagement in metacognition and whether this correlates with attainment. What about when researchers deliberately teach students to engage more in metacognition? Hattie et al. (1996) conducted such a review which found that study skills were effective, but warned that beyond simple mnemonics, they may not always transfer from one subject to another. Accordingly, this and other research studies (e.g. Bransford et al., 2000; EEF, 2018; Pintrich, 2002) have since argued that studying is not composed of generic transferable skills but works best when embedded into curriculum areas and specific tasks (although schools could also do both).

Dignath and Büttner (2008) reviewed a broader set of attempted interventions around study skills and learning to learn and found significant effects with high effect sizes, especially in some curriculum areas. This suggests that metacognition has a large impact (effect size means the size of the difference in mean scores, such as percentage scores on a test). Benefits were found for both secondary and primary school students; this is useful, as it suggests that metacognition need not be considered out of reach of younger learners (and other research has suggested that, in other contexts, metacognition can at times compensate for cognitive difficulties or weaknesses; Veenman et al., 2006).

Some other interesting findings from the Dignath and Büttner review included the following:

- Effect sizes for mathematics performance were higher at primary than at secondary school, while for reading/writing performance, they were higher at secondary than at primary school;
- Studies of strategies with primary school students were higher if the intervention was done individually rather than in groups;
- Across all age groups, effects were larger if there were a larger number of training sessions and if training was conducted by experts.

These findings concord well with more recent research, though other researchers have been more positive about the benefits of metacognition outside of maths contexts. Slavin (2013) found that metacognitive interventions were among the most effective approaches to improving attainment in both reading and maths. And based on a review of science education, Avargil et al. (2018, pp. 45–46) stated that metacognition "is correlated with robust and profound scientific understanding, the ability to read scientific texts, effective learning strategies, and problem-solving skills".

The Issue of Student Engagement

At times, the potential benefits of metacognitive strategies may be undermined by students' willingness to use them. The use of strategies may conflict with a student's broader self-regulation of their learning, their approach, and their emotions. In particular, Boekaerts and Corno (2005) describe how wellbeing and metacognition can come into conflict. If a student places an emphasis on their wellbeing, they may choose flawed strategies, because more effective strategies often feel challenging (see also Bjork & Bjork, 2011). However, if they do engage in more effective strategies, this can trigger a virtuous cycle, where greater attainment and increased motivation reinforce each other.

This inter-relation between emotions and metacognition strongly suggests that, for attainment, emphasising strategy would be a more effective approach in schools than trying to reassure or motivate students in other ways. There is also evidence that the impact is strongest when interventions focus not just on one metacognitive strategy but on several (Muijs & Bokhove, 2020).

Overall, the evidence suggests a significant and positive impact of metacognition on attainment, benefits that apply across the curriculum and to all ages. Metacognition has more of an effect when students are specifically trained and when several strategies are covered, but this must be put into a curriculum context by a knowledgeable teacher rather than relying on generic 'study skills' guidance. This is the approach advocated throughout this book.

Different from Other Interventions?

To return to a point raised in the introduction to this book, some educators might ask "Why metacognition?" The more cynical might even wonder if it's the latest educational fad. As someone who has been engaging with research into psychology and education for decades, I think there are good reasons to think that it is not.

Firstly, many of the fads that people may be aware of have always lacked the kind of research support that accompanies metacognition. Concepts like learning styles (see Chapter 6), though widespread in education, never had strong support from psychology researchers, while others such as 'Brain Gym' or the 'Mozart effect' were largely driven by commercial interests, not research (and many cognition researchers were oblivious to these ideas!).

In contrast, metacognition has now been the focus of decades of research, albeit as part of a field that took off later than research into reading or memory, for example.

The process and models are now well understood and widely accepted by mainstream education researchers, and we have very helpful theories that suggest practical strategies. And while research into metacognition is challenging to conduct well, it doesn't rest on a plethora of flawed studies, as is the case with some other concepts (e.g. multiple intelligences; see Ferrero et al., 2021).

Also, unlike some of the concepts mentioned above, there isn't really any debate among researchers about whether metacognition exists!

Whom Will This Help?

As we have seen, metacognition research has been conducted in many age groups and curriculum areas, and there is no curriculum area to which it can't be applied. Granted, like anything else in the classroom, some metacognitive strategies will take time and motivation. Some strategies are complex, too, and the concept as a whole takes a while to wrap your head around. It also needs to be presented to students in an age-appropriate way. However, the foundations can be put in place even with very young learners. The benefits of engaging with metacognition are therefore likely to apply to most educators in a vast range of roles.

Even before tackling some of the specific strategies that are explained in later chapters, the teacher may find it useful just to increase learners' awareness that they can learn how to learn. Students are often astonished to discover that there are a set of strategies that they can apply to get better at tasks. They often naively assume that success in areas like writing or maths is just a matter of ability. For this reason, many students are quick to see the value of metacognition, and engage with it enthusiastically.

There remains a major question about the extent to which teachers are able to assess their students' metacognitive skills accurately (Muijs & Bokhove, 2020). If we don't know it when we see it, then it can be hard to gauge whether intervention is necessary. But a key message throughout this book is that we can engage with metacognition more, with our awareness, knowledge, and practical skills all growing in unison.

Concluding Comments

In this chapter, we have explored what researchers mean by metacognition and considered what a metacognitive approach to teaching would look like.

I know that readers will be in a hurry to explore some of the strategies that can be put into place in the classroom. That will, of course, be a major focus, starting with some of the simplest and quickest in Chapter 3 and then moving on from there to some more specific, task-focused strategies.

However, metacognition can be undermined by how difficult cognition is to understand. To appreciate the fundamentals of metacognition, and promote it successfully in the classroom, teachers need to understand memory. Therefore, we will next – in Chapter 2 – take some time to explore the intricate and often deceptive nature of memory and how it underpins both learning and metacognition.

Discussion Questions

What do you think the key arguments are for a metacognitive approach to teaching?

Can you think of any further examples of processes that happen at the metacognitive level? Are there any processes that are hard to categorise?

What is your starting point – for example, what is the level of metacognitive knowledge among your students and staff at present?

2 | The Shifting Sands of Memory

Imagine you are sitting down in a classroom, ready to learn about a brand-new topic. You feel engaged, curious, and ready to learn. Great! You're an excellent student, the kind that any teacher would be lucky to have.

The class begins with an explanation of how parliament is elected. The teacher explains political parties, election of specific candidates, and the need for any party or grouping to attain a majority of representatives.

You are nodding; some of this seems familiar, other parts are new. And when the teacher asks you a few questions, you are able to answer them confidently. As you leave the room at the end of the lesson, you're pleased that you have really learned something about politics and the role of a citizen.

If an observer (such as member of senior management) was in the classroom, perhaps they would comment that the lesson was well structured with high-value curriculum content and that the students seemed engaged and answered the questions correctly.

Everything is fine.

But wait – two months later, you have an exam. To your dismay, you realise that you greatly struggle with the sample questions found on the exam board's website. You didn't take many notes during your lesson on elections, and what you experienced is now very hazy in your memory. As you revise, it starts to feel like you are re-learning the entire thing from scratch!

If the above scenario sounds familiar, you're not alone. In this chapter, we will see how being a metacognitive learner (and a metacognitive teacher) helps to turn good-but-flawed classroom practice into teaching and learning with a lasting impact.

We will begin by exploring how learning works and its underpinnings in long-term memory. You will come to see some of the flaws in the above classroom example and how we can consider such situations not as 'learning' but rather as temporary performance, easily forgotten.

Armed with a better understanding of learning and forgetting, you will be in a position to make better *metacognitive* decisions about how lessons should proceed.

DOI: 10.4324/9781003386971-3

Performance vs. Learning

It's certainly very tempting as either a teacher or a student to assume that getting answers correct means that you have 'learned' something. However, many psychologists disagree. To understand this, bear in mind that the entire process of a lesson in school has been scaffolding the student's behaviour and understanding. In the example above, the teacher has just spent the best part of an hour giving students guidance, hints, and reminders. With everything fresh in their mind, it's not surprising that they can get most of it right.

However, we probably don't want to say that something has been learned until students can produce the knowledge or skill without this help and scaffolding. Our real question should concern not whether they can do it *today*, during or at the end of the lesson, but whether they can do it in a few months' time, out of context, and without a reminder from the teacher.

The temporary improvement we see within a lesson or study session is more accurately termed 'performance' rather than 'learning' (Soderstrom & Bjork, 2015). Throughout this book, I will refer to the terms performance and learning in this sense. It's really important to understand the difference, so let's take a moment to explain this a little more fully.

(Oh, but first, mark this page. Bear in mind that your own metacognitive understanding of learning is still developing in a very similar way. If you feel you understand the difference between performance and learning now, that doesn't mean that you'll have retained it successfully enough to be able to explain or apply it in future…).

It's worth pointing out that performance is not the same as working memory (also known as short-term memory). That particular system lasts for only around 30 seconds and holds just a tiny amount of information – for example, seven random words (which is why students can become cognitively overloaded). Working memory therefore can't hold everything that you engage with during a lesson or a private study session, and it can't retain things until the end of that session, either. It certainly can't keep things in your mind until a test or exam!

So, in fact, even performance does draw on long-term memory. (Don't worry – I'll say more about the difference between working memory and long-term memory later.) The problem is that performance reflects an emerging, fragile, poorly interconnected impression in long-term memory. The memories have not been fully embedded, as this is a process that takes time and practice. They are therefore highly susceptible to forgetting (again, more on this in a bit).

Some examples of learning situations where we may observe performance rather than learning are the following:

- A student's ability to answer questions on material where they read about it, heard a teacher explanation, or watched a video just a short time before;
- The way that you can recall a hotel room number throughout a holiday but forget it within a few days or weeks of returning from your trip;

- The detail that we remember from a book or movie immediately after engaging with it (over the longer term, we may not only lose familiarity with details and specific scenes but also forget the existence of some major characters);

- Strategies, techniques, and game plans learned during a sports training session being forgotten as a learner returns to bad habits developed previously.

Now, remember that this book is about metacognition. In all of the examples above, the problem is not *just* that someone might forget something after initially practising it, though that is problematic in itself. There is an additional problem – the fact that they might be totally unaware that this forgetting (or reduced performance) is going to happen.

That is to say, students may incorrectly *believe* that they have learned something. And when someone believes incorrectly that their learning is effective, they may continue engaging in flawed practice and fail to course-correct (Kornell & Bjork, 2007).

It's therefore important that learners come to realise that their performance is only temporary and get used to doing certain things to transform that performance into learning.

Tasks 2.1 and 2.2 ask you to consider some of the implications of the performance-vs.-learning distinction.

Task 2.1

Most of what we observe in practice is not permanent learning. Ponder on that idea for a moment!

Take a minute or two to write a short response to the idea. What are your thoughts on the idea of temporary performance? What are the implications for planning, teaching, or observation of lessons? What about for developing student teachers?

What kinds of things might we need to do in order to support permanent learning?

Task 2.2

In an experiment, researchers Koriat and Bjork (2005) gave learners weakly associated pairs of words such as "basket–kitten" to study.

They then asked the learners to predict how they would do if tested in the future. For example, they might be asked, "If we show you the word 'basket' in future, will you remember the word 'kitten'?"

The researchers found that participants significantly overestimated their ability to remember in the future when prompted by one of the cue words. They described this as an 'illusion of competence'. Participants thought they had learned the pairings, but what was happening was actually fragile, temporary performance.

Considering the research study, have a think about how this could happen in classes, too. Can you think of examples of when learners have confidently stated that they know something, underestimating forgetting and overestimating their own competence? Perhaps you can think of examples of when you yourself were sure that you knew something, only to fail to recall it when it really mattered. Write these examples down in your notes.

Looking back at the Politics class described at the start of the chapter, you might now be more wary as a learner (or as a teacher) about whether the 'good practice' was effective. Yes, the class were engaged, the material was interesting and well presented, and in your role as an (imagined) student, you got most of the answers correct. But did *learning* actually occur?

In fact, from what we have seen, all we (or an observer) can really see is performance. And while it's impossible to see learning over such as short timescale, the general approach taken in class is geared more to performance than to learning.

Fortunately, learning is not a complete mystery to scientists. In fact, there are a set of very well-established and evidence-based techniques that can be applied to boost learning in any educational context. Let's look next at some of the most valuable and flexible of these, and consider what they mean for metacognition, too.

Desirable Difficulties

In their seminal paper on performance vs. learning, psychologists Nick Soderstrom and Robert Bjork point out that the things that feel easier and make progress quicker are often worse for learning, not better (Soderstrom & Bjork, 2015).

Things that feel harder during study tend to be avoided by students. After all, who wants to feel that their learning process is going slowly and arduously and that they are making a lot of mistakes? It's not surprising that people avoid difficulties.

Accordingly, students will tend to study in flawed ways – ways that are too easy. And professionals, too, are subject to the same illusions (Firth, 2021; Halamish, 2018; McCabe, 2018). Most tend to think that easier options are better.

Specifically, there is a widespread preference for learning strategies that involve the following:

- Making rapid and straightforward progress;
- Studying over fairly compressed timescales;
- Low levels of errors during the learning process;

- Fairly passive learning, where information flows from the teacher to the student;
- Covering one topic at a time in a predictable context.

Research has shown that all of the above strategies are less effective ways to learn. In contrast, to be more effective and to promote learning rather than performance, we should be seeking to make progress slower, more spread out over time, more error-prone, more active, and more varied.

These things have come to be known as *desirable difficulties* because they make learning harder but more effective. There is, in fact, evidence that goes against all of the common preferences listed above:

- Making learning more challenging rather than too easy is more effective. One way to do this would be to ask a student to stop and summarise a text or video rather than simply to read it. Doing so would be slower, but they would learn more from it (van der Zee et al., 2018).

- After initial practice, it's best for topics to be re-studied at least three widely spaced intervals (with gaps of days or even weeks between sessions) rather than topics being covered in a single day (Rawson & Dunlosky, 2011). This is called the spacing effect (see Case Study 2).

- It's a myth that errorless learning causes mistakes to become habitual (Metcalfe, 2017). Instead, it's best for learners to challenge themselves with difficult questions before, during, and after engaging with new material and to accept errors as part of the process. If they are making no mistakes, the task is too easy!

- We may conceive of learning as students getting information from a teacher or a book, but, in fact, forgetting is greatly reduced when they actively retrieve from their own memory. This is known as retrieval practice and can take many forms, from a quiz to a debate. Information taken in from a text or video is more rapidly forgotten, even where learners encounter it more than once (Agarwal et al. 2021; Roediger & Karpicke, 2006).

- Rather than keeping tasks as predictable as possible, variation is a desirable difficulty. What happens if study proceeds in multiple locations and multiple formats and if skills are tried in multiple contexts? Things get slower, yes, and more mistakes are made, but knowledge and skills are also more resilient and more easily transferred to new contexts. That is to say, the process better meets the definition of 'learning' (Soderstrom & Bjork, 2015).

These examples should already begin to illustrate how the Politics class described earlier could be taught more effectively. Questioning could be pitched at such a level that rather than answer all the questions correctly, the students would struggle at times. Rather than posing them all in today's lesson, some could be delayed to a later date. And so on.

23

Most teachers won't realise these issues spontaneously. The tendency is to assume that if the class are working well and enjoying the lesson, everything is going fine. And the headteacher and students won't know either. Everyone assumes that learning is progressing well, but yet, far too much will be forgotten by exam time, leading to students feeling that they are starting almost from scratch when they revise.

These points also illustrate a major idea that you will encounter throughout the book: learning is not intuitive. We can't rely on what feels right (to either ourselves or students) when deciding how to teach or how to study. Intuitions lead us astray. Part of becoming a metacognitive practitioner, then, is engaging with the evidence on how learning works and applying these ideas to our planning and our practice.

Task 2.3

The points on this page emphasise how the practitioner should be guided by evidence rather than intuition or assumptions. Is there a particular point or quote that you'd like to highlight? Note this down, along with one or more references to a research study that you'd like to look into more.

In addition, have a go at summarising the role of intuition and assumptions in education in your own words. What issues have you noticed among your students and colleagues?

Now let's build on the idea of desirable difficulties by explaining what actually happens when we learn something new. How does information enter memory in the first place – and what causes it to stay there or to be forgotten?

The Process of Learning

Everything that we learn must be retained in memory (Kirschner et al., 2006), and for that reason, this book will refer to memory (especially long-term memory) quite a lot. However, it's probably clear to you that memory and learning are not exactly the same thing. So, how do they differ?

A useful analogy that I sometimes use is to see memory as being like our muscles and learning as being like running or playing a sport. That is to say, you need memory in order to learn just as you need muscles to move. One can't be done without the other, but they are not the same thing. Rather, one is a system that underpins the other.

Our students are not trying to put things into their memory – they are trying to learn. But in order to learn, we can't get away from the fact that memory systems are necessary. Nothing can be learned without first being processed in and by our memories.

It's therefore valuable to have some initial idea of memory (an understanding which is metacognitive for you as the practitioner, as it involves thinking about and understanding learning. In this case, a teacher's metacognition involves understanding the *cognition* that happens when information enters memory and is processed).

A Simple Model of Memory

Many people see memory as progressing something like this:

1. New information hits your senses.
2. You pay attention it, causing the information to flow (somehow) into your working memory – a kind of small pot that can hold only a few words.
3. Despite those words in a pot being entirely unconnected to anything you have learned before, you somehow turn them into a new fact or 'schema', thereby transferring it into permanent memory.
4. There it stays unless you are unlucky enough to forget it at some point.

It's probably obvious that there a few important omissions from the steps listed above. We have already encountered the idea of desirable difficulties such as spacing and variation, and these are absent from the above simplistic version of the memory process. However, let's assume for a moment that the four steps outlined are largely correct and complete. A visual representation of this idea can be seen in the diagram below, a representation known as the *modal model* of memory (Figure 2.1).

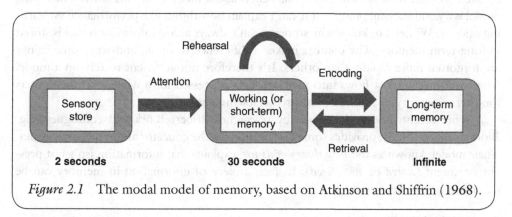

Figure 2.1 The modal model of memory, based on Atkinson and Shiffrin (1968).

Despite its simplicity, the modal model can help to set out some useful principles for the teacher. Most important among them is that if no attention is paid to new information, it won't enter memory at all. If we are distracted or fail to notice something, the key information will fade fast from the senses and won't be processed in working memory.

This may happen if a student is supposed to be reading a text or listening to their teacher but gets a message on their phone instead. This part, at least, is intuitive – we tend to realise that we failed to notice or pay attention to something.

It's also true that working memory has a very limited capacity, as mentioned earlier. It can't maintain more than a few words or ideas in working memory at one time, and these will fade very rapidly unless students work to retain them.

Additionally, the model is pretty accurate in saying that things generally won't enter long-term memory if they aren't first processed in working memory. However, the opposite is not necessarily true – being processed in working memory doesn't guarantee entry to long-term memory. This is an avenue for misconceptions; students may assume that because they spent some time thinking about something, reading it, or listening to the teacher, the information has been learned. As explained already, such classroom experiences will often lead to *performance* rather than permanent learning.

The modal model of memory is therefore rather over-simplistic, something that reflects the fact that it was developed before a lot of the ideas discussed in this chapter were discovered. The basics of the model are not fundamentally wrong; most psychologists agree that systems such as working memory and long-term memory do operate in more or less this manner and order. However, as a theory (and one that dates back to the 1960s), it lacks detail and nuance.

A More Accurate Model of Memory

As part of the focus here is on your metacognitive understanding as a teacher, we of course also want to make sure that your beliefs about memory are *accurate*. The modal model is a good starting point, but it can't explain how things like performance vs. learning operate. We need to know why students can't always access information that is stored in long-term memory, why context makes a difference to recall, and why some things are forgotten more rapidly than others. It's therefore not sufficient to rely on a model where information just flows into memory, gets processed for a while, and then enters long-term memory in a more or less predictable manner.

A more recent model, developed by researcher Robert Bjork and colleagues (e.g. Bjork & Bjork, 2023), provides some clarification for the educator about these key issues. Their model, known as the *new theory of disuse*, explains that information isn't just present or absent (*stored* or *not stored*). In fact, a piece of information in memory can be described by two key variables:

- Storage strength
- Retrieval strength

This means that a fact about parliament (for example) can be easy to retrieve but poorly stored, as in the case for something that the learner just heard about in class five minutes ago. Alternatively, it could be well stored and hard to retrieve, as may be the case for facts you learned at school but haven't thought about since.

Hopefully, you can see that thinking about memories in these slightly more complex ways helps us to tackle the realities that we see in classroom situations like the one described at the start of this chapter.

The researchers have further explained that some of the more ineffective methods of study, such as re-reading a text immediately, boost retrieval strength but not storage strength. They make a memory more accessible but not more well learned (in the sense of being lasting and transferrable).

Meanwhile, desirable difficulties boost storage strength but not retrieval strength. They don't always make things easier to retrieve in the here and now (some, like spacing and variation, can make this harder). But they help to make that information more well stored in the long term. This means that the information will be less likely to be forgotten and that it will be easier to transfer to new situations in the future.

Congratulations – your metacognitive understanding of memory and learning is growing fast! And hopefully you are starting to see why it's so important that this metacognitive understanding is accurate. Case Study 2 shows an example of how these concepts can be applied in practice.

Case Study 2:   The Animal Kingdom

Hector is a primary school teacher. His class have been learning about the animal kingdom, and today's focus is on the biology and habitat of species of birds. At the end of the class, students are getting every answer right, even when he picks individuals at random to answer. They have also done some impressive writing and drawings, labelling birds and using the correct terminology.

However, Hector has been reading about memory. He realises that the accurate responses he sees in class today reflect performance, not learning. In order to tackle this, he resolves to actively test some of the key information the following day. The morning's lesson will begin with a review quiz. Students will be asked to answer questions in a different context and order than before. Where they answer questions with ease, Hector sets a follow-up 'why' question, aimed at helping them integrate knowledge and make links.

Hector also begins to tackle forgetting via homework. In the past, he would have given out homework straight away, and usually pupils completed it that night and brought it into class the next day. However, Hector now realises that delaying this practice should be useful. He adopts a schedule of setting homework based on a topic from three weeks before.

Comment on Case Study 2

The example of Hector in the case study shows how understanding memory phenomena is not purely abstract or 'just for interest'. These ideas can be implemented immediately in teaching.

We can also see that planning plays a key role. Homework tasks can be scheduled later rather than immediately, allowing for the benefits of delayed consolidation – the spacing effect. This doesn't require any new materials to be created or any change in time or workload for either the teacher or the student (Firth, 2021).

Hector has also developed a keen awareness that immediate responses shouldn't be trusted. These don't indicate permanent memory. By incorporating desirable difficulties such as a delay, active testing, and variation of the context, Hector's follow-up task will help the material to stick in memory, and he is also seeking to elaborate and deepen their meaningful understanding via the 'why' questions. The next section of this explains the importance of a rich, interconnected understanding.

Schemas and How Things Get into Memory

The idea of the schema may seem abstract and difficult at first, but it is very useful for the practitioner to know about. The essential idea is that information is not stored in our minds as separate items or files (as is the case in computer memory) but is taken in and stored in memory in interconnected bundles, with new information linked to what was learned before. In this respect, the human mind is unlike a computer.

When learning about a rare kind of tree, for example, you would probably want to know whether it is similar to other kinds of trees with which you are familiar. You might think to yourself, 'Oh, it's like a rowan tree but its leaves are slightly different'. This kind of thinking shows how new information is being connected to and influenced by existing knowledge.

An implication of the ideas above is that new knowledge builds on old. Some research-ers would put this idea even more strongly – that the thing that most influences new learning is what the learner already knows (Ausubel, 1968; Bransford et al., 2000; Wiliam, 2011). Most teachers are probably already aware of the value of finding out students' prior knowledge and current understanding. This fits well with cognitive psychologists' understanding of how memory (especially the schema concept) works.

Schemas also have a social and cultural element. A schema for an everyday object might be relatively universal, but many schemas depend on our upbringing – schemas for a family meal, for a school, for a wedding. Even a tree is interpreted differently depending on culture. To one person, it's a source of shade or firewood. For another, it's a garden decoration.

Although there are certainly differences among how people from different cultures perceive or think about objects and events, it's easy to overstate this and ignore the great similarities in how we think and learn. Most of our learners, regardless of upbringing and culture, respond to most objects in remarkably similar ways. However, it's worth being aware that slight biases can exist and that these can lead to misunderstandings.

And even schemas for things that appear to be matters of objective fact can depend on cultural values. Consider, for example, how people take in new information about vaccines. If they are part of a subculture of vaccine deniers or conspiracy theorists, they may categorise new information very differently from how most learners would. Their intake of new information to memory is biased by social views and values. We don't categorise things into schemas logically and objectively. Again, the human mind is not like a computer.

Task 2.4 explores the schema concept a little further.

Task 2.4

An interesting demonstration of how culture can bias memory dates back to the work of Bartlett in the early 20th century. One of the first people in the UK to study memory scientifically, Bartlett (1932) discovered that how people remember the details of pictures and folk tales was biased by their culture.

More recently, researchers have suggested that the knowledge that a learner brings to the learning situation will fundamentally affect their ability to do tasks such as reading a text (e.g. Hirsch, 2003; Moll & Gonzalez, 1994).

For this task, find a text that you have used with learners. It could be quite short, like a scenario in an exam question, or something longer. A set of instructions on a worksheet could also be used. If it's a longer text, the first page or two should be enough.

Now, underline or highlight each item for which you think the learners may be using their schemas to understand the text. You will quickly find that you are underlining quite a lot! Bear in mind that schemas include all of our beliefs about the world, including actions as well as objects.

Finally, for at least one example, note down at least one way that different learners might have differences between their schemas due to prior learning. Is it possible that this could affect overall understanding or lead to slightly different interpretations of the text? Note down your thoughts.

Schemas and Student Metacognition

When we begin to explore some of the more abstract mechanisms involved in cognition and memory, you may find yourself wondering whether to share this information with learners. And certainly, as we will see throughout this book, part of benefiting from metacognition will involve activating learners as self-aware and self-regulating.

However, it may also occur to you that some of these ideas would be much too hard or too complex for them to understand. That's fine. There is a complex science behind memory, and as with any area of science, we wouldn't expect learners (especially younger children) to take it all in straight away, to tackle topics that they are not ready for, or to do things that are far too difficult.

To take the example of schemas, I *do* explain this to practitioners, as it captures a complex idea perfectly. While it may take time to fully understand, I feel it's important for educators to work towards a view of memory that is accurate and comprehensive. This means appreciating the way that memories are structured and the effect that this can have on student understanding and misconceptions.

The same argument could be made with students. However, they are *not* professionals and don't have a responsibility for education beyond their own learning. While they will certainly benefit from understanding that new ideas don't enter their memory directly and that prior assumptions can affect what they recall, it may well be appropriate to present a simplified version of these ideas, perhaps without mentioning the term 'schema' at all. (See more about metacognitive talk with learners in Chapter 3.)

As an analogy, consider that what we tell school students about a healthy diet may be very different in terms of both detail and terminology compared to what you would read in a scientific article about nutrition.

As we go forward, then, it will be useful for you to consider your own learning context and the extent to which there will be a gap between your professional knowledge and what you expect of students. There will be ways that you can simplify things, especially for younger students.

The Unreliability of Memory

The final aspect of memory that educators really need to know about is how unreliable it is. It's not just forgetting that is the problem here. In fact, nearly everything that goes into memory is modified and actively reconstructed when we try to recall it. This idea follows on directly from the concept of schemas and is in fact an implication of how memories are structured and stored.

To take a famous example of flawed memories, many people have a clear and vivid memory of a particular historical event. They may feel that this memory is so clear it's like a photograph in their mind. Psychologists call this 'flashbulb memory'.

For decades, confidence in the accuracy of these memories was assumed to be well founded, but more recent evidence has found that people's confidence in their own memories is sharply out of line with the accuracy of these memories (Marsh & Roediger, 2013). For example, a few years after the 1987 *Challenger* space shuttle disaster, researchers Neisser and Harsch (1992) gathered data on people's recollections and found that the large majority of subjects had major inaccuracies in their memory of hearing about the news, such as their location, the activity they were doing at the time, and who told them. Around a third of participants were wrong on all three of these aspects.

The evidence on flashbulb memories shows another metacognitive error. Not only is memory prone to inaccuracies, but what people believe about the accuracy of their own memories is apparently unreliable as well.

More broadly, none of our memories is really a fact. We are not replaying memories like rerunning a movie or slideshow (even though, again, this is often how people think about memory). Memory is a more like storytelling – a creative, constructive process. When recalling something, we take a group of ideas which are stored with varying levels of storage strength, along with cultural knowledge from our schemas, and build something that appears to make sense.

This process fools people into thinking that their memories are more accurate than they actually are (a problem when questioning eyewitnesses in legal cases!). If you have ever had a conversation where you and another person can't agree on what happened or what was said, it's likely that both of you are being honest about your recollections – it's just that you remember the same events differently (and it's quite possible that both of you are wrong). This again shows the unreliability of memory. Task 2.5 invites you to reflect on this idea.

Task 2.5

If you previously thought that someone saying, "I was there, and I remember" was a convincing statement, do you feel quite as sure about this now?

Consider how this might apply to your practice. How certain can you be about what you recall from a class or from a learner's work? How might that affect things like reporting on students or discussions with colleagues or parents? Are there processes you could put in place to make your recollections more accurate?

The reconstructive nature of memory means that people's memories can be biased in very particular ways. Most importantly, they can come to incorporate false information received after an event (such as an error heard in a group discussion) or ideas from schemas (Wells & Loftus, 2013). In the classroom, this could involve the following:

- A student's prior assumptions biasing and distorting their recall of a factual information, such as what they heard about a historical or political event;
- Students filling in the gaps about what a teacher said (e.g. in relation to rules or safety);
- A student believing that they have been told one thing about their exam requirements when in fact they were told something else.

What's more, some of these biases and distortions in memory happen after a period of time. Some experiments have looked at flawed or false memories, finding that these crop up after days and weeks. And critically, people usually have no awareness that their memories are flawed.

This means we need to be very wary about student confidence in their own learning and recall. It is very hard to rely on students' assumptions about what they remember. In this context, it's easy to see that asking questions such as "How confident are you on this topic?" is a flawed approach. Instead, we need to get *evidence* of what they remember, to do so after a delay, and to check for common misconceptions.

Concluding Comments

In this chapter, we have explored some of the fundamental features of human memory and seen how they can lead to metacognitive errors among students. It should now be clear that the intricate and counterintuitive nature of memory can lead us astray and that a metacognitive approach to teaching will make students aware of this issue and guide them towards smarter choices about how to learn.

Now, it's time to look at some of the specific techniques we can use to tackle the challenge of flawed metacognition.

Discussion Questions

How would you describe the link between memory and learning?

Do you agree that we currently focus too much on performance (rather than on learning)? Can you think of any practical examples of this?

What areas of memory would you like to learn more about?

3 | Low-Hanging Metacognitive Fruit

The previous chapters have shown that people don't automatically understand how learning works or how to make use of their own memory system effectively. Because of this, many students will study ineffectively, making bad choices when it comes to both classroom learning and independent work.

However, it's not all bad news. We've also seen how metacognition is closely linked to attainment. What's more, it involves a set of skills and strategies that are very open to improvement (Rivers et al., 2020), in part because they are based on (metacognitive) knowledge. This means that unlike in some aspects of education, it's possible to see rapid changes if we target the right things and begin to take a metacognitive approach to teaching.

In a 2012 article for the *Journal of Applied Research into Memory and Cognition*, psychologists and memory researchers Henry Roediger and Mary Pyc discuss inexpensive techniques to improve education, with a focus on better use of memory. In their paper, they note that many educational initiatives are very expensive to implement and have debatable benefits. In contrast, they argue, applications of the cognitive psychology of memory are sure-fire (they apply to everyone), inexpensive (they don't require any special apparatus), and effective (Roediger & Pyc, 2012). They conclude that techniques such as desirable difficulties are *low-hanging fruit* – easy wins for the teacher, there for the taking.

In this chapter, I present another crop of low-hanging fruit – metacognitive techniques that are likewise easy to do and almost cost-free and that can be used by any educator. They are simple and under our control.

What's more, such techniques won't just benefit learning in the here and now, but if they are implemented as part of a metacognitive curriculum, they can set our students up to be more successful self-regulated learners over the long term (see Chapters 8 and 9 for more on this issue!).

Our focus here, then, is on quick wins – easy things that any teacher can put in place in their classroom right away.

As I was writing this chapter, I tried to think about what I would do within the first month if I were moving to a new school and working with students who had never heard

DOI: 10.4324/9781003386971-4

of metacognition before. The strategies presented are highly practical and straightforward to implement without lengthy training or extensive background knowledge. They relate to the general running of the class; later (in Chapters 4–7), we will zoom in and look in a more granular level at tools that can enhance specific classroom activities.

Professional Focus

Even before we delve into the classroom strategies, the first thing that any teacher can do is dedicate some professional focus and time to understanding metacognition and to exploring its potential to support their learners. This means a certain commitment, which you, the reader, are displaying by reading this book so far and no doubt through many of your other activities.

As a quick win, clearly you can't immediately read everything there is to know about metacognition! The point here is to make a commitment. Just as some people might target running a marathon but recognise that it will take time and effort to prepare, this is about committing to becoming a metacognitive practitioner.

You can start to cement this commitment by talking about metacognition to colleagues and making it known that you intend to make metacognitive strategies part of your professional practice (or, at least, fully and open-mindedly try them out). In doing so, you will increase the chances of peer support and help to establish a culture of metacognition-informed pedagogy in your classroom and beyond.

It's also important to start talking to your students about this! It will be a lot harder for students to benefit from metacognition if they are unaware of its existence. Some of the strategies in this chapter involve encouraging 'metacognitive talk' and preparing students for certain changes to classroom norms.

An interesting starting point, at least for some groups of students, could be to present metacognitive knowledge as a missing set of instructions regarding how to learn. (See Case Study 3 for an example of how this could be done.) This can help students to see that metacognitive strategies can make their learning and school experience easier and boost their success.

Case Study 3:   A Thinking Learner

It's a new term, and Ms. Bartlett has just taken over a class in her new primary school. Through discussions with other staff over the holidays, she has learned that there is currently no systematic education on how to learn in the school, and that the approach to study skills that the students have experienced so far has not been informed by theory or evidence.

Aiming to make this fun and accessible, she spends some time presenting the story of a learner called Jann, who has been doing well at their lessons. Jann, Ms. Bartlett tells the class, is a *thinking learner*. They know how to learn well. How did Jann get this way? The class are invited to suggest their ideas!

She proceeds to tell the class the story of how Jann found a set of instructions on how to learn. Jann had been doing badly at school and thought of themselves as stupid. Reading the instructions, Jann realised that everything they needed to do in school was explained in the instructions! At one task after another, Jann got better and better at their learning.

The class become curious to know if Jann's instructions are real. To make this more fun, Ms. Bartlett creates a set of ancient-looking scraps of paper with handwritten texts about learning. She explains that scientists in far-off lands created these instructions but that it's going to be necessary for the class to piece them back together. Over the coming weeks, students occasionally find another part of these mysterious instructions and start to piece them together on the classroom wall like a collaborative jigsaw.

Comment on Case Study 3

The scenario described in Case Study 3 won't suit every context. For some learners, a more direct approach will go down better, whereas for others, it could be made even more fanciful – perhaps students could be asked to come up with creative stories for how Jann found the instructions.

Either way, the essence of what Ms. Bartlett said is accurate. Metacognition can be seen as a set of instructions for how to learn, it is relevant to every task, and it can transform a student's approach. It's even true that this knowledge was devised by researchers around the world.

The jigsaw added another level of fun and curiosity, but again there was a serious purpose to this professional choice. This class wouldn't be able to take in new metacognitive strategies all at once, and the gimmick allowed Ms. Bartlett to present insights one at a time. The idea of students constructing a jigsaw out of what they learned was a metaphor for their becoming self-directed learners but also encouraged them to think about how each new strategy connected to what had gone before.

While researchers have emphasised the benefits of developing accurate metacognitive vocabulary, this has to be age-appropriate, and it's fine to make a judgement call on the right time to use the term metacognition (if you do so at all; see Chapter 2). Ms. Bartlett chose the term '*thinking learner*', which is a near synonym. Other terms could also work, but it's best to avoid neuroscience-inspired synonyms such as 'brain-based learning', as these unhelpfully put an emphasis on biological explanations of learning.

Foundations

We will now look at classroom strategies that can help to form the foundations of metacognitive teaching and learning as well as establishing essential routines and norms that will get learners ready for strategies covered later in this book.

Thinking Aloud

The teacher is metacognitively the most sophisticated individual in a typical classroom, but their accurate and expert thinking about the subject matter is often hidden. It remains private – silent, inside their head. A straightforward solution is to talk more about what you are thinking while you teach (e.g. when demonstrating a task). This is called *thinking aloud*.

The goal of *thinking aloud* is to share and model your metacognitive processes with the class. As a class work through a task, your voice can provide an excellent example of how to do things like come up with a new idea, decide what strategy to use, check for facts, make a link between two things, or simplify a problem. This also helps to show that thinking about thinking is a normal part of successful learning.

For example, a teacher could show a scenario-based maths problem on a screen and talk through their own approach to solving it, step by step. They could also estimate the answer before beginning, modelling some of the metacognitive control process that come into play for expert learners.

Teachers can also draw attention to common problems and pitfalls, discussing how students would avoid these or course-correct if things go wrong. This helps to model that thinking and reflecting are useful throughout the learning process. (Further examples relating to *thinking aloud* are explained in Chapters 6 and 7.)

Scaffolded Stems

A strong level of agreement has emerged among researchers that it is beneficial to develop the language to engage in 'metacognitive talk'. Do learners have the capacity to discuss their own learning, including the vocabulary to do so accurately? Of course, this will depend on the class and particularly their age. For some classes, particularly with younger students, you might explain the concept in a different way, such as talking about being 'thinking learners', as was done in the example in the case study (see Case Study 3).

It's helpful to consider the vocabulary needed to discuss learning as being very like the vocabulary needed to discuss science. It doesn't emerge overnight, but by early secondary school at least, students can be expected to know the core terms. We can also scaffold their use of language in order to help them get started. The *scaffolded stems* strategy means guiding students towards some of the statements needed. This can link to thinking aloud, responding to mistakes, or any other metacognition, and in each case, students take the stem and add more detail. Stems might include the following:

- A mistake I commonly make is...
- When working on this topic, I have learned not to (rely on)...
- My goal is to learn more about...
- I have always wondered...
- My weakness with project work is to...
- An easy mistake to make is...
- A problem I had recently was... and now I know that I should...

This scaffolding could be done orally, or a teacher could provide sentence stems in a written form, such as a handout, a poster on the wall, or a table to paste inside a notebook. To keep the order more fluid and the format dynamic, they could be written as a set of flashcards instead and perhaps shared among a table of students.

The *scaffolded stems* technique will make it much easier for students to start talking fluently about their own thinking. Like other scaffolding, the help can be gradually withdrawn over time.

Task 3.1

Two key points to get across to learners are (1) learning is a skill and (2) we can't rely on the accuracy of our current beliefs about learning.

Note these down and then consider how you might emphasise and reinforce them. Could they be displayed on your classroom door, for example? How would you encourage or scaffold metacognitive talk about these?

If you can, share your thinking about this with a colleague or online.

Misconceptions Corner

Students also need to be warned about the metacognitive errors that most people are prone to. Their naive understanding of learning is likely to be very flawed, and it's important to tackle this. Using the *misconceptions corner* strategy brings the focus fully on one specific misconception at a time, raising awareness of issues and debunking myths. One misconception could be tackled at the start of the week, for example. A chosen misconception could be based on subject matter (such as common missteps in a maths strategy) or on learning more generally.

Researchers have found that misconceptions can be hard to overcome, in part because they are interlinked with a very cohesive, common-sense understanding of the world (Bryce & Blown, 2023). In this context, misconceptions may pop up repeatedly and need to be corrected more than once. This can be done gently, of course, but it's important to tackle errors head on rather than relying on students making inferences (Will et al., 2019).

As part of *misconceptions corner*, you might ask students to predict or estimate how a particular cognitive process works. This is a form of pre-testing, in itself an effective, evidence-based learning technique (see Richland et al., 2009). This can align well with your own professional reading; you may happen upon a surprising finding that you want to share with your class(es). Task 3.2 also points the way to some suitable choices.

Task 3.2

Drawing on the ideas in Chapters 1 and 2, develop a list of the misconceptions that you especially want to target. This could be done collaboratively with colleagues.

Now, take some time to consider when you will tackle each one. Will you tackle one per week, for example, or would a less frequent schedule work better in your context?

Finally, consider when you will return to the misconceptions. In line with the spacing effect (see Chapter 2), we can't expect learners to retain things perfectly without delayed practice. A good approach to consolidation would be to engage learners in a creative task after every four or five misconceptions, allowing them to summarise the ideas, make links, and perhaps share the ideas with other classes.

(See also the 'Pop Quizzes' section below as an example of a task that embeds metacognition via delayed practice.)

Five Bees

Another foundational practice is to support learners in becoming less reliant on the teacher. This is a win-win; it makes the teacher's role easier as we are not always being asked questions, but also forces learners to become more self-regulating and to think more about what they can do alone.

Five possible sources of support can be summarised by the '5 Bs' (or *five bees*) mnemonic. In order, the 5 Bs are

1. Board: Is the relevant information or instructions displayed on the board/screen?
2. Brain: Can you actively recall what you need to know, perhaps from what was said in a previous lesson?

3. Book: Try looking for the required information in your booklet, textbook, or handout.
4. Buddy: Speak to the classmate that you sit closest to. They may be able to give you a reminder of instructions or peer-teach the required concept.
5. Boss: If all of the above approaches fail, then, of course, the student can ask the teacher (i.e. 'the boss') for help.

It would be simple enough to display these strategies on the classroom wall, meaning that when a student asks a question, simply pointing to the mnemonic could be enough to get them back on track. Bear in mind, though, that this is another form of scaffolding. As with other aspects of metacognition, the support could be removed when students are working this way more automatically, without prompting.

Point out that the same strategies also apply to homework; if students are really stuck, there comes a time when they will need to ask for support, but to do so, they can't leave homework until the night before.

Classroom Skills

Experienced teachers develop a set of go-to strategies that become almost routine during their day-to-day teaching. These things often don't need advance planning. Instead, teachers notice a situation in the classroom and react accordingly. The following strategies fall into this category.

Spontaneous Connections

There is broad agreement that engagement with metacognition will ideally connect to everyday teaching rather than coming through stand-alone study skills sessions (see Chapter 1). A tricky but valuable strategy is for the teacher to spontaneously point out when cognitive processes are taking place, again using accurate terminology and prompting metacognitive talk.

The *spontaneous connections* strategy is hard to do well, not just because some such examples may occur unpredictably but also because there's so much else for a teacher to keep track of during a busy class! You may simply fail to notice. However, this is balanced out by the fact that cognitive processes are happening all the time, every minute of every day in the classroom. There are plenty of opportunities. And when processes are highlighted, it acts as a clear, meaningful, and memorable example for students. These frequent, everyday links make it much easier for students to see the relevance and breadth of metacognition.

The following quote by Paul Pintrich (2002, p. 223) expresses very well how *spontaneous connections* could be used during a lesson focused on reading and shows the use of metacognitive talk too:

> the teacher can note occasions when metacognitive knowledge comes up, such as in a reading group discussion of different strategies students use to read a section of a story. This explicit labelling and discussion helps students connect the strategies (and their names/labels) to other knowledge that they may already have about strategies and reading. In addition, making discussion of metacognitive knowledge part of the everyday discourse of the classroom helps foster a language for students to talk about their own cognition and learning.

Post-It Reminders

In the 'Spontaneous Connections' section above, I pointed out that it can be tricky for a teacher to notice when cognitive processes are taking place. One way around this is to make it a habit to write down two or three relevant connections on a Post-it note and add them to your lesson plan or materials or simply stick them on the whiteboard (a digital Post-it note on a slide could also work!).

Granted, they won't include examples that arise unpredictably, but they will have the benefit of being well thought out and relevant to the lesson's objectives. The Post-it will provide a hard-to-miss reminder, prompting you to comment on them when they arise during the lesson. And if you *still* forget to cover them, it's not a major problem. Unlike missing a key bit of curriculum content, it doesn't matter especially if you don't make the link with metacognition on one occasion, as there will be opportunities to make a similar point in the future.

Pop Quizzes

Learning is a cumulative process; gaining new knowledge is more like adding to a network than filing away a separate item (see the discussion of schemas in Chapter 2). Accordingly, knowledge affects other knowledge. When we circle back to prior learning, it prepares students for further learning, makes links across different parts of the curriculum, and helps them to recognise what they know.

A great way to ensure that this happens is to start using *pop quizzes* frequently. These are brief tests, low stakes and not announced in advance. Before presenting a class with new information, set a quick quiz on prior learning from a few days ago or a few weeks – or a mixture!

A quiz involves retrieval practice (see Chapter 2) and is therefore more effective than a teacher verbally repeating this content (which is more passive). *Pop quiz* questions work best if they are short-answer, multiple-choice, or true/false. But the simple nature doesn't mean that this is all about surface learning. Used in this context, quizzes facilitate deeper connections.

When teaching a class on rainforests, for example, you might ask students a set of questions about animals, plants, and weather, linking to topics covered earlier in the year. As well as readying students and facilitating links, *pop quizzes* can help to tackle forgetting, as they occur days or weeks after the initial lesson. This is the spacing effect in action – a desirable difficulty.

Crucially, though, *pop quizzes* also help to raise awareness of metacognitive processes. When asked tricky questions on things that they knew well before, students begin to notice gaps or errors in what they thought they knew well. They come to see that their knowledge is less secure than it should be! That is, the challenge inherent in such tests helps to raise students' awareness of forgetting.

The difficulty of recalling past content can sound stressful, but evidence suggests that students don't experience this as a negative (Agarwal et al., 2014). It may even be reassuring, as they gain a more realistic idea of what they know well and what needs to be practised further.

Powerful Purpose

"No wise fish would go anywhere without a porpoise."

– Lewis Carroll

How many times in your school days did you get told to do a particular activity or exercise with no discussion about why you were doing it? To quote Lewis Carroll, perhaps we should be asking about the porpoise... sorry, the *purpose* of the task.

Why students are doing a task in the first place is certainly discussed too little. It may be implicitly assumed that this is good for their future or necessary for an exam. The *powerful purpose* strategy is about being more specific, going deeper, and asking students to reflect on what their goal is and how they will know when they have achieved it. As such, it helps to make the learning process more obvious to learners as it happens.

This could be done through brief quiet reflection, via writing, or via discussion. It would be a suitable moment for a 'think-pair-share' activity.

For many tasks, particularly written ones, thinking in detail about the purpose could also connect with a discussion of the audience (or marker) who will read the work. Who will read your poem, for example, and what do you want them to think or feel when you do so? Engaging in this form of metacognitive thinking is recognised as being part of the skill of a sophisticated writer, although it does take time for this capacity to develop (Kellogg, 2008; more on this in Chapter 7).

Sharing learning objectives with a class does go some way towards this goal, but it's important that this isn't just a mechanical process ("Everyone, please copy today's LO off the board…"). Instead, it should prompt learners to think about what they are about to do and how they will judge success.

This strategy can also be used to raise students' awareness of a metacognitive purpose. For example, perhaps you tell them about the spacing effect. Then, when you return to a topic and do further practice after a delay of a month or so, a discussion of the *powerful purpose* should (hopefully) lead to students recognising that delayed practice is both effective and necessary. It could also lead naturally into further discussion of how memory works; you may point out, for example, that when we engage in spaced practice, the longer the delay is, the bigger the impact (Cepeda et al., 2008). Metacognitive purposes could be displayed visually (see Task 3.3).

Task 3.3

The phrase above could be a quote for your classroom wall: The longer the delay, the bigger the impact! What other quotes about memory and learning could you put up in service of raising awareness about metacognition? And how will you present these?

Take a few minutes to scan through this book and perhaps to look back at other texts you have read on metacognition. Begin to make a list of useful quotes and think about what to do with them. Perhaps you can make a dedicated space for learning insights in your classroom. If so, consider including space for students to comment on any such quote with questions or with their own examples.

Pointful Planning

Some planning is rather pointless; at times, it would be better to get on with the task without delay. However, if you want students to think more, they will need time and prompting to do it. A useful habit is to allow a little more time than is customary for silent planning at the outset of classroom tasks or to take a break for *pointful planning* five or ten minutes after beginning.

When students are new to it, this will work best if scaffolded with a few questions to think about, such as the following:

- Think back to a previous time we did a task like this. What did you find challenging?
- Consider and/or write down what you want to gain from this task.

- There is more than one way to do this task. Think about which strategies you might use today.
- What will you do if this task isn't going well?

Hopefully, over time, students will be able to think deeply and metacognitively about these questions, such as by reflecting on past learning, setting goals, selecting strategies, and identifying sources of support (see the 'Five Bees' section above).

When you are just starting out, responses to *pointful planning* might not be very sophisticated, but even asking students to stop and think helps to raise awareness that it is worthwhile to consider how to approach a task before you begin. In a similar way, they could also be prompted to pause and reflect mid-task (see Chapter 4 for more on this). As they get more experienced, planning and doing become more fluid and recursive, at which point a briefer *pointful planning* session might be best.

Tracked Thinking

Keeping a careful record book or spreadsheet with every student's attendance, test scores, and homework performance. Does this sound familiar? Many teachers take great care over keeping records of their students' performance on a range of tasks. But how careful a record are the students themselves keeping?

In line with increasing ownership of learning (see above), *tracked thinking* involves asking them to keep a careful record of their own test scores and progress. Doing so will provide a nudge, inevitably leading to some metacognition, and (hopefully) a stimulus to improve.

Better still, invite students not just to keep a record of grades/marks but also to spend a few minutes writing a comment on each one. Why do they think they underperformed on week 12's homework? This needn't be secretive; they could discuss with classmates to find out more about how others have improved their performance.

Working Together

Metacognition is not purely an individual process. Just as we can use language to think and create together (Mercer, 2000; Sawyer & DeZutter, 2009), peers can also help by prompting, scaffolding, and feeding back on metacognition. Our emphasis on grades in education often appears to demand confidentiality or even secrecy, but for metacognition, it really helps if at least some of the discussion of thinking comes out into the open and if students or groups take the lead. The following strategies work towards those goals.

Think-Pair-Share-Care

Many teachers use the think-pair-share (TPS) technique to raise the level of students' thinking prior to a group discussion and to leverage peer learning. TPS is helpful to metacognition as peers get the opportunity to hear a partner's reasoning for their ideas or answers prior to sharing with the class as a whole, and where there is disagreement, each partner can briefly make an argument to support their view.

A way to enhance TPS is to add a fourth stage where each student briefly writes some feedback for their partner. I liked to call this stage 'Care', partly because it rhymes (making it easier to remember) and partly because the benefit is mainly for the partner's learning, so it is a caring, prosocial activity.

The format of *think-pair-share-care* could be as simple as dividing a Post-it note in half and writing a positive comment on one half and a negative one on the other (see Figure 3.1 for an example). Better still, explicitly direct your students to make these metacognitive comments by asking the class to comment on their partner's thinking or learning (again, whether or not you use the word 'metacognition' will depend on the context and stage you are at) (Figure 3.1).

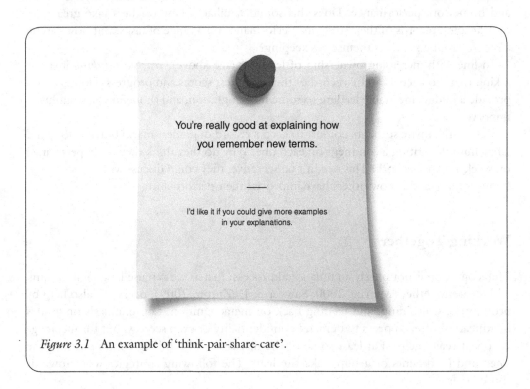

You're really good at explaining how
you remember new terms.

———

I'd like it if you could give more examples
in your explanations.

Figure 3.1 An example of 'think-pair-share-care'.

The *think-pair-share-care* strategy will elicit some very rapid and personalised metacognitive feedback, which can become increasingly accurate with practice.

Learning Survey

Students can be asked to survey their peers – either in a group or the whole class – to ascertain more about the ways that people are going about aspects of learning, including homework, revision, and projects. A *learning survey* of this kind may helpfully tie in with the development of research skills, connected to an authentic purpose.

From a metacognition perspective, the *learning survey* strategy is a good opportunity to raise or reinforce the issue of a lack of insight into our own thinking. It helps to clarify and make concrete that a learner doesn't always understand their own learning or accurately recognise their own strengths and weaknesses. Seeing it in others will help students to appreciate this limitation in themselves. Hopefully, though, you will also start to see evidence of the techniques you have worked on being adopted.

A teacher may choose to share with the class the outcome of these surveys or have students take ownership of this, giving mini-presentations to each other or at events such as parents' nights. Teachers and students alike could track the use of certain study habits and approaches over time, looking for trends towards more evidence-backed approaches to learning.

Map Reading

An important way to prompt more metacognitive thinking among students is to get them to take more ownership of their learning overall. *Map reading* is an analogy – consider how active reading a map is, in contrast to listening to directions from your phone. As a more active task, *map reading* forces the individual to think about where they are going and how they are going to get there. This applies not just to an actual map but to any learning task.

This may be an uncomfortable proposition for professionals who prefer lessons to focus on teacher-led direct instruction, but the more students make decisions for themselves, the more they are forced to think about their goals and reflect upon their progress. If your temptation is to step in when something is going wrong or to nudge a learner towards that small next step, it will involve disciplining yourself with a certain restraint. As an analogy, this observation applies to parenting as well as to teaching (consider the notion of 'helicopter parents', unwilling to let their children make mistakes).

In practical terms, *map reading* can involve a 'less is more' approach, where you minimise help and instructions. Of course, young people won't transform into self-directed learners overnight. At first, it may be a case of gradually dialling down the extent to which you are on hand to help. (This combines well with the *five bees* strategy described above.)

At the more extreme end of the scale, some educators have advocated for the 'silent way', where a teacher says nothing at all, leaving the students to work out what to do and whether they are doing it right from body language alone (e.g. Gattegno, 1963). Without suggesting this as a broader goal for teaching, it does help to illustrate the potential of building up students to map-read – to set their own goals and figure out what to do next. And especially as students get older, the emphasis in education will become more strongly focused on self-regulated learning, where there is no teacher to give instructions (see Chapters 8 and 9).

Plenary Poster

A plenary section of a lesson plays an important role in consolidating new content and skills, but it has a metacognitive element too. During a plenary, students' awareness is raised of what they have learned and why, how their classmates are progressing, and what they still need to do.

However, this is largely implicit in most classrooms. For a more metacognitive plenary, you may wish to direct learners more specifically to think about their own thinking and to use metacognitive language. That way, they come to know what they know and to recognise which skills and processes are happening.

A *plenary poster* is a poster or diagram on your classroom wall (though a slide would also work) which scaffolds this visually. Usually, it's a form of support that you provide, but over time, students could come to have an input in the *plenary poster* or even take charge of it completely. Items/prompts on the poster might include the following:

- What were we trying to learn today?
- What strategy did we use?
- When did things get difficult?
- What did we learn?
- How confident and certain are we about our progress?
- Next steps?

As mentioned elsewhere, the scaffolding provided through this strategy may cease to be necessary as the concepts and skills become more internalised. Initially, though, the *plenary poster* focuses students on their learning and highlights the potential benefits of using feedback and reflection as a learning strategy. See Figure 3.2 for an example of what a plenary poster might look like.

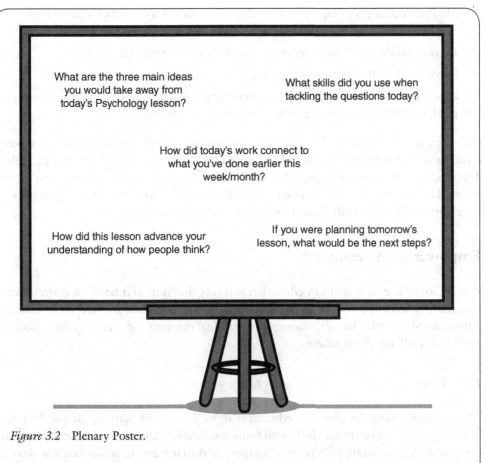

Figure 3.2   Plenary Poster.

This example shows a plenary poster as used by a Psychology teacher in a secondary school.

Metacognitive Norms

Peers are an important influence of behaviour, and in part this operates through the establishment of social norms of behaviour. Norms are formal or informal ideas of accepted ways to think and act, and they can influence academic outcomes, particularly when the norm connects to a social group with which students identify (Reynolds et al., 2015).

In your classroom, consider how you build *metacognitive norms*. Is there an effort to support thinking about how students learn, while refusing to accept more mindless or routine approaches? This could include the following:

- Drawing attention to metacognitive role models (including yourself – see 'Thinking Aloud' section above);

- Mixing student grouping up so that they hear examples of metacognition from outside their own friendship group;
- Directly tackle the drive to memorise without understanding;
- Directly tackle the motive of focusing on grades;
- Promote talk about why learning is useful beyond purely instrumental motives (e.g. getting into the next class/college/university/not failing).

However, it's also useful to be aware that these *metacognitive norms* will be more powerful if students identify with the group (Reynolds et al., 2015; Terry & Hogg, 1996). Therefore, using inclusive language, emphasising holistic group identity ("we as a class are working towards this"), and avoiding labelling specific individuals or sub-groups (e.g. "the boys don't like revising") will make this strategy more effective.

Empowering Assessments

While a lot of the time spent in education involves the 'nuts and bolts' of learning new material and skills, at times the focus shifts to assessment and testing. Here, too, metacognition can play a role. In fact, assessments are ideal prompts for metacognition because goals and feedback are so salient.

Prep Time

There is an ongoing discussion in education about how much warning should be given before tests. Practitioners may feel (with some justification) that tests without prior warning give a more accurate picture of attainment and that warning students a few days in advance leads to cramming. Certainly, in the right context, a snap test may provide the teacher useful information. But for more embedded learning, preparation will be a process. The *prep time* strategy is all about getting learners to think ahead and consider how they will prepare for an upcoming strategy. Advance warning may also help students to remain calm and make good choices under pressure.

There are different options for how this time will best be structured and used, and it may be valuable to try different variations in your own setting. The best plan may depend on the age of learners and the nature of the tests, too. However, ideally, we want to move away from cramming and towards having *prep time* – time to ensure that students are ready for tests via an extended embedded process, and one where they take some ownership.

Supervised Notes

The process of making revision notes is often left to the students themselves. In some ways, this may seem to fall in line with the call for better study skills elsewhere in this book (e.g. see 'Map Reading' section above; Chapters 8 and 9). However, teachers may be missing a trick. Why have students revise from notes, flashcards, and so forth without checking the quality of these materials?

Supervised notes involves taking some of this process into the classroom and allocating time to it. Teachers could spend some time showing students how to write a good flashcard (it appears that most students don't use flashcards effectively; Agarwal & Bain, 2019). Blank index cards could be provided. In terms of students' long-form notes, in many cases they will have taken these during classes, and there may be errors and omissions. A bit of scrutiny while preparing for a test can help students avoid trying to revise from inaccurate information!

The process of preparing and revising in class in a supervised way helps to provide some basic training in these skills. As students become more confident, the time will certainly come for taking the water wings off and letting them swim for themselves. The key, then, is recognising that note-taking is a skill and not throwing learners in at the deep end. (There's more on note-taking in Chapter 9.)

Guesstimating Performance

There are two main points at which researchers tend to ask learners to estimate their performance: before an assessment and immediately after taking the assessment. This approach can be mimicked in the classroom, for example, when teachers ask students to keep a careful record of their test scores.

The *guesstimating performance* strategy involves asking students to make specific estimates of their scores, which can later be compared with their actual performance. This way, they are getting feedback not just on how well they attained but on the accuracy of their own metacognition. This strategy combines very well with *tracked thinking* (see above) – students can be asked to note down their estimates alongside their actual grades.

Precision Feedback

Some teachers like to give unrealistically negative feedback in order to motivate learners to work harder. And while that may serve a purpose, feedback that is both precise and accurate – *precision feedback* – is much more helpful for metacognition. Learning in school and college contexts often has a slow feedback loop between learning and course outcomes (see Chapter 6), especially for older learners. Grades and comments from the teacher are valuable as interim feedback.

Precision lies in the level of detail. In the early days of my primary schooling, I remember receiving feedback saying 'good' or 'very good' on pieces of writing and pondering over the distinction between these two terms. Such holistic feedback is unclear to learners, and percentages are not much better unless it is clear how the score was derived.

49

In contrast, situations where it is obvious that a particular flaw led to a particular loss of marks make it much easier for a learner to course-correct.

Lemov (2019) gives the example of how teachers using this method can use clipboards during teaching to keep precise notes of where students are going wrong – circulating the room and updating this accordingly. This leads to a precise record of where errors are made. Without such data, sharing 'common mistakes' with the whole class is considerably less impactful.

This strategy again combines well with *tracked thinking*. Students can be asked to take time to summarise feedback in the notebooks or trackers, along with their grades. See also Task 3.4.

Task 3.4

Several of the strategies mentioned so far include an element of scaffolding, whereby you might need to provide detailed guidance at first but gradually remove this support.

In your notes, make a table with two columns. In the left column, list what these strategies would look like with scaffolding, and in the right column, note down what the same strategies would look like after they have been practised and embedded.

Select whichever strategies you like for this task – focus on the ones you are most likely to use. Leave space for adding more strategies later!

Feedback Folders

A common complaint among teachers is that students look only briefly at their feedback on homework or tests and then cast them aside. Colleagues are right to suspect that such minimal engagement is likely to have little effect. The use of *feedback folders* as a strategy tries to extend the discussion and the reflection by filing away feedback (or photocopies) such that students can access it regularly.

Often, especially when receiving a poor grade, students' immediate reaction to feedback is rather defensive. They may be embarrassed or simply want to stop talking about it as soon as possible. Others may have done well and feel proud of themselves or want to compare with classmates. These reactions are all natural enough, but none of them assists with learning. Instead, it's necessary to prolong the focus on what students have learned from an assessment. And, of course, we can't rely on their memories of how they performed! This is what makes *feedback folders* so valuable.

To make the most of this strategy, teachers may wish to schedule in time to speak to students individually or in small groups. To prepare for these discussions, students could be asked to spend 10–15 minutes looking at the documents in their feedback folder and select a few key points that they feel they need to work on. This task in itself prompts metacognition. In subsequent discussion, the teacher not only can demonstrate how to engage in effective reflection but also can flag up pitfalls. It will also provide some expert scrutiny to ensure that students aren't missing any important targets in their review of their own feedback.

Assessment Wrappers

Several of the strategies above focus on discussion and preparation before an assessment takes place and, of course, on reflection afterwards. A way to tie these things together is known as an *assessment wrapper* (also called an 'assessment sandwich'). The goal is to emphasise assessment as an extended process which involves not just testing but also planning and reflection.

A way to make this more concrete for learners is to provide a worksheet or checklist that they can use to keep track of their progress towards the assessment and actions afterwards (more scaffolding! See Task 3.4).

Many of the other strategies discussed earlier in this chapter can tie in well with the use of *assessment wrappers*. For example, using *scaffolded stems* before and after assessments can prompt students to think not just about how they did but also about what went well and where they could improve. In line with *thinking aloud*, time could be taken for teachers to model how to tackle questions where students tend to struggle, and classmates could be encouraged to talk through any errors with a peer.

Concluding Comments

In this chapter, we have looked at some of the quick wins (or 'low-hanging fruit') that metacognition offers to a teacher. The intention was to present a set of strategies that could be put into place more or less straight away in any classroom. If metacognitive practice is quite new to you, hopefully you can see that despite its theoretical basis, it is in fact highly practical. The benefits are within reach to all practitioners, and we can start to work towards these benefits without a huge amount of time and preparation.

The strategies discussed so far are quite general. How can we build metacognition directly into specific classroom tasks? This is the focus of the next three chapters, which place an emphasis on planning (Chapter 4), on monitoring (Chapter 5), and on reflecting on one's own learning (Chapter 6).

Discussion Questions

Which of the strategies in the chapter would you find most useful to implement?

Which strategies, if any, are you already using?

How do you think your students would react to these strategies? Could you see them adopting 'metacognitive norms' over time?

In the Classroom, pt. 1
Before the Task

The previous chapters have outlined the basis of a metacognitive approach to teaching as well as sharing some of the quickest and most general ways that any teacher can start implementing this approach with their learners. If you have taken these steps, you are already well on your way to being a metacognitive practitioner!

Now, it's time to dive into the specifics of how this would be applied on a more granular level, focusing on the various tasks that make up most of a student's lessons or day. In doing so, we will explore three key phases of metacognition which have been widely discussed in the research literature on metacognition and self-directed learning. These connect to the idea that the thinking (both cognition and metacognition) that a student engages in for any learning task has different phases: before, during, and after the student engages with a task (Nelson & Narens, 1990; Zimmerman, 2000).

Three Phases of Metacognition

As a simple example of what the three phases of metacognition might look like, consider a student writing a Geography essay. They should plan the essay (before). They may then think about how things are going as they write, such as whether their points are relevant and if they are generally on the right track (during). Then, subsequent to handing the essay in, they may reflect on whether they fulfilled the goal of the task or wonder about what grade they will get (after).

This structure concords well with the metacognitive strategies mentioned in the previous chapter, which include planning for learning (e.g. *pointful planning*) and reflection (e.g. *plenary poster*). However, while those strategies focus on general classroom approaches and teaching skills, the focus here is on enhancing specific tasks.

It's worth bearing in mind that the impact of metacognition often extends beyond the classroom. Later chapters will pick up on some of those wider issues (e.g. in relation to self-regulated learning and project work). For the next few chapters, the focus will be on our students' ability to anticipate and plan before they commence a classroom task, on

DOI: 10.4324/9781003386971-5

their ability to recognise issues as they learn, or on their ability to reflect accurately after each task is complete (sometimes also called a 'plan–do–review cycle').

Task 4.1

Consider the popular strategy 'think-pair-share' (see Chapter 3 for a variation of this). Could the three stages of this be seen as mirroring the *before*, *during*, and *after* phases of other tasks? If so, are there ways that these stages could be more clearly structured or more explicitly linked to metacognition, so that students get more from them? Note down your thoughts.

Before the Task

We spend so much time in education thinking about exercises and assessments that it's easy to forget how much thinking – and therefore work – happens before anyone puts pen to paper.

Think back for a moment to the last time you tried an academic task of some kind, such as writing an essay or article or attending a lecture. What happened before you began? What did you do or think about? What did you expect to happen? What information were you given, and how did you interpret this? Whom did you talk to?

The answers to these questions begin to unlock some of the metacognitive processes that happen before a task even begins. Your own experiences will have parallels in the classroom for students of all ages. What you will have realised is that *you don't just start*. You inevitably think about your own learning, at least a little, before you begin.

There is a good cognitive reason for focusing more on the planning phase of a task than is often done. You may be familiar with the concept of cognitive load; this is the idea that human working memory (the part of your mind that does thinking and processing) has a very limited capacity. When we are in the middle of a task, working memory is essentially 'full'. There's little or no space for planning (or for modifying a plan). This means that it is worth making sure that key ideas are considered in advance and perhaps noted down where learners can keep track of them as they proceed through the more complex phase of a written task, exam problem, debate, and so on.

However, for many students, planning is very brief and informal. They may take a few seconds to decide what strategy to use for a mathematics problem, for example, and then begin trying to solve it. If there are instructions, or key background information in a textbook, they may skim read them briefly or not do so at all.

In some ways, this is like trying to build furniture without the instructions. The failure to think about *how* you are going to do a task before you begin can cause the outcome to be worse and the process to take longer.

The solution? Given that we know that many students are likely to be impetuous and keen to get going without delay, we can speculate that they are unlikely to engage in a thorough planning stage unless this is prompted or structured by the teacher. The emphasis, then, is on the teacher to build this into their lesson plan.

Extended Plans

Part of the answer to the problem is simply to allocate more time to planning. After all, you are the teacher. You get to decide how much of a lesson's time is devoted to the planning of a task and how much to the doing.

The *extended plans* strategy means just that – giving more time and emphasis to the process. Exactly how long the planning should last is difficult to say in general terms because it depends so much on the learner and on the task. However, it's likely to decrease as expertise increases. Experts are not entirely above the need to plan, but they have partially automated many of the key elements required, leading to a skilled (but often uncreative) performance (Gube & Lajoie, 2020). What an expert may need is a nudge in the right direction, prompting them away from the tried and tested strategies (see 'Try a different way', Chapter 5).

Sometimes, when thinking and planning, people feel that they have run out of ideas. However, there is evidence from the technique of brainstorming to suggest that better ideas come later in a planning session and that it is worth persisting (Deuja et al., 2014). For tasks that involve creative thinking (e.g. planning an essay or a science experiment), it's likely that enough time is usually not given to achieve the best results. Students should keep planning even when they think that they have no more ideas and should be encouraged to reject earlier ideas in favour of ones that come later. As with creative thinking, it can be a messy process!

Other types of task will be much quicker to plan. When using *extended plans* for a short answer or thinking about the strategy for a maths problem, even an extra 1–2 minutes may be longer than the norm.

Thoughtful Structure

Planning may seem boring to students if all you are telling them to do is sit and think about how they are going to solve a maths problem, carry out an experiment, write a geography essay, take notes on a video, or whatever.

For this reason – and to avoid planning starting to be seen in a negative light – providing a *thoughtful structure* can help to make things more fun and engaging. The *thoughtful structure* strategy involves drawing their attention to the specific things that they should be doing while planning, and it's called 'thoughtful' because metacognition is all about thinking about learning!

Sometimes, the *thoughtful structure* will involve directing students to a specific outcome expected from the planning stage, even if this just means taking some notes or talking to a partner about how they plan to solve a problem. You might choose to use a planning sheet to scaffold their plan, or you might otherwise engage them in using some type of visual representation. In science writing, a funnel metaphor is widely used; the introduction to an essay or report begins broad and general and gets gradually narrower and more specific as the piece goes on. This is a form of *thoughtful structure*, and students could also write a more extended plan based on this metaphor, perhaps with a printed template to help. A piece of writing or a science practical could be planned as a flow diagram.

At other times, students may take general notes, but even then, a *thoughtful structure* will be helpful. If you want them to note down things to include in their essay, for example, why not ask them to write things under headings that align to their paragraphs rather than just writing on a blank sheet of paper? Practice of shorter exam-type questions could be structured around the marks available; for example, if a student is thinking about an eight-mark question, they could write down eight bullet points and try to note down how they aim to get the marks for each one.

Of course, there are tasks where it may seem like overkill to write a plan. If a student is going to dive into a Mathematics or Physics problem, perhaps the main thing they need to do is figure out one or more suitable strategies for solving it. However, even here, there are areas where the provision of a *thoughtful structure* would help them to think deeply before they get 'into the weeds'. They could be given some reminders of the kind of pitfalls that they personally have experienced before. Common questions or issues could be shown on a wall or in their jotter. For example:

- Start by listing everything you can see on the map segment, leaving a gap under each one to add details and analysis.

- Don't forget to round to two significant figures.

- Are you going to need to use cos, sin, or tan? Think about this in advance and use a mnemonic if you need to.

- What variables might affect the motion of the object? List them all before you start.

This strategy can also help to develop a metacognitive understanding of *why* students are doing a task, something that Bransford et al. (2000) argue is often neglected. For example, they note that most students believe that maths is about computation; in contrast, they describe the role of a more metacognitively focused maths teacher in promoting understanding. The teacher in their example, Magdelene Lampert, begins a task by prompting a class discussion of possible solutions: "My role was to bring students' ideas about how to solve or analyze problems into the public forum of the classroom [and] to referee arguments about whether those ideas were reasonable" (Lampert, 1986, cited by Bransford et al., 2000, p. 166).

Above all, during the planning phase, it should be clear to students what they are supposed to be doing and how they should do it. They should have some indication of the time that will be allocated and the expected outcome. Even if they are only expected to sit and think silently, the *thoughtful structure* strategy helps them to know what they are supposed to be thinking about.

It's worth noting, in line with the previous strategy (*extended plans*), that planning can be messy. Encourage this messiness. If students are very drawn to writing plans neatly, point out that the initial thinking benefits from a degree of chaos and from changing your mind. They can always write a neater draft of their plan afterwards.

Group Planning

Some writers have raised concerns about the use of group work, as it can lead to freeloading and to incorrect information being shared (Salomon & Globerson, 1989). However, even bearing these limitations in mind, there can be some real benefits from planning in a pair or group.

Consider a case where high school students are going to write a practice exam answer, perhaps taking around 15 minutes to do so. Common practice would be to start the clock immediately and assume that they would do some planning during the allocated time. There's nothing wrong with that, and it closely mimics the exam situation. However, what students don't get in that situation is a chance to learn from each other.

The *group planning* strategy helps students to think about and avoid pitfalls before beginning. What flawed assumptions did your partner make? How does the A-grade student that you are sitting next to plan their essay? Even just hearing a student say something like "I always start with a definition, and I always get a mark for it" could raise awareness or remind students of something that they were told before by the teacher but had forgotten.

Hearing others talk about a question and having a chance to get brief feedback on one's own approach can also boost confidence – everyone likes to know that they are on the right lines before they begin. Activating peers as learning resources for each other is one of the five key formative strategies recommended by Wiliam (2011) and others, and this is an example of how it can also boost their capacity to engage in another of these five strategies – activating students as owners of their own learning. *Group planning* helps to achieve this.

Overall, allocating even just a few minutes for a group to discuss how they would go about an essay could be a highly efficient way to keep learners on track rather than having to unpick problems later.

Activating Prior Knowledge

Prior knowledge plays a major role in any learning (see Chapter 2), but there can be barriers to students using it effectively. The *activating prior knowledge* strategy tries to ensure that students think about what they know and use it strategically.

One barrier is that many students fail to see the relevance of their prior knowledge. Many have life experience and skills that they fail to bring to bear on a task. Young children, for example, have many everyday experiences with numeracy but sometimes struggle to connect these to classroom contexts (Bransford et al., 2000). Later, we will look at an example in another strategy (see 'Key Comparisons' section in Chapter 5) where learners didn't recognise the relevance of a problem, even though it had been provided shortly before.

A straightforward way of *activating prior knowledge* is to build it into a starter task. Many starter tasks are designed to be fun and motivating, and many reflect back on and consolidate prior learning (e.g. via a pop quiz; see Chapter 3). However, starters also serve to look forward, activating relevant schemas. A metacognitive element can be added to this by asking learners to predict how this might be useful in the tasks they do today, perhaps via very open questions such as

- "Now, what do you think that last task was leading up to?"
- "We just looked at X. Can anyone think how we might use that knowledge later today?"

Even these questions may not always be enough for learners to draw the apparently obvious links between their starter and main task, so don't hesitate to drop further hints as you move through the lesson.

Plan for Homework

We've seen it so many times on US television shows that it's become a cliche: the teacher yelling the homework assignment as the students rush from the room! And while most of us are much more careful and methodical in setting homework, it remains the case that students often get told *what* to do but receive relatively little guidance on *how* to do it. They note down the assignment or access it via the school virtual learning environment (VLA), and then... they just have to get on with it.

The *plan for homework* strategy tackles these issues and makes the most of the expert input of the teacher prior to homework being undertaken. In line with the broader training in how to learn discussed throughout this book, we can equip students with strategies to tackle their work. At least in the early years of school or when students are new to a subject/topic, they will benefit from the chance to *plan for homework*, readying them for the point when they have to try it alone. This scaffolding can gradually be withdrawn, but it may be required again during later stages of schooling when they face new subjects and a more complex set of tasks.

Consider the use of times tables and reading and spelling tasks in primary school, for example. How much time in class is spent talking about how memory works, when it's best to practice, or how long to leave before returning to something? In the absence of such training, students' intuitions (or those of parents) are likely to lead them astray (Pan & Bjork, 2021).

One example where a form of *plan for homework* is already widely done is the 'look, say, cover, write, check' approach used in early reading. When students know what to do, and practice it carefully in class, with support, they are better able to apply the same strategy at home (and they understand what it is for). In other areas, however, intuitive approaches to learning at home may focus on repetition or cramming rather than spaced practice. In line with the points made in Chapters 1 and 2, students won't make effective choices unless we show them what to do. As part of training in how learning works, the *plan for homework* strategy can start early, providing a strong foundation for later, more complex tasks (Firth, 2022).

More broadly, telling students how to do something will be a lot less effective than showing them how to do it. For that reason, a great way to *plan for homework* that should take (for example) 30 minutes would be to spend the first 10 minutes in class. This will greatly reduce confusion, stress, and time spent by students (and often parents) trying to figure out what they are supposed to be doing.

Visual Planners

Visual planners are ways to support students' thinking via diagrams and other visual cues.

I often recommend the use of a 'target diagram' for the planning of written tasks, though it could be used for other contexts, such as field work and debates. The idea is to write a diagram with concentric circles, rather like an archery target. Students should then note down the most relevant points in the central circle and progressively less essential points (though still ones that they might want to include) in the circles further out.

This process helps students to think about which items, if any, they may drop due to time or word count constraints. The target diagram can therefore continue to be useful as they proceed into the task itself.

There is no need to obsess over getting the diagram perfect. Sometimes, writers will change their mind about the relative centrality of ideas as their thinking develops. This process provides a form of formative feedback on their planning, potentially refining and speeding up later planning.

Other forms of *visual planners* could include the 'funnel' for scientific writing mentioned earlier (see 'Thoughtful Structure' section above) as well as mind maps, spider diagrams, and so forth.

Case Study 4: Fieldwork

Chris has been carrying out fieldwork in Geography. He has gathered some data on rock samples and now wants to write up his findings. His teacher has guided him towards certain tools for writing in the subject, some of which have been practised in previous classes. For example:

- A flow diagram showing the format of a lab report
- A target diagram to help with prioritisation.

Chris sits down late in the evening to begin work but doesn't make much progress. He finds it easy to get bogged down in the detail of his findings, and all of it seems equally important!

The next day, in class, he looks at it again, with some input from his teacher, Miss Lorenzetti. The teacher sets the students a task to explain their findings in simple terms to a classmate. She then suggests that Chris simplify his planning, tackling one section of the write-up at a time and using a target diagram to focus on that section. Chris makes faster progress but also sees that this will be a time-consuming process.

Discussion of Case Study 4

It is apparent from Case Study 4 that, even with planning tools, an extended writing project is not a simple matter. Scientific writing involves organising and analysing data and using this to make a coherent point. Chris tried to use some of the suggested tools but found them overwhelming.

The teacher wisely encouraged Chris and his classmates to focus on the main message that they wanted to get across. She then overcame the potential confusion of multiple tools and strategies by getting Chris to focus on one section of his write-up at a time.

This case shows that often, 'less is more' with planning tools. We can see from Case Study 4 that Chris did have some experience with using the tools, but he still struggled to make progress with the work independently. Here, more modelling and scaffolding of the process in class made more sense than having students struggle fruitlessly.

In addition, by the end of the class, it was apparent that Chris had a more realistic metacognitive judgement of how long the task would take and was more prepared to tackle it one section at a time.

Planning as the Task

At times, it will suffice to give students a little bit of planning and thinking time – just a few minutes, which may already be more than would typically be expected before they jump into the task itself (see 'Extended Plans' section above). In other cases, however, planning is likely to be complex. It requires the mastery of certain skills and may have more than one phase. The *planning as the task* strategy emphasises that the plan itself can be a task worth focusing on.

Consider, for example, an extended homework task such as an essay or project. These could be tasks that students are allocated several days to do. In such cases, *planning as the task* would mean that the plan could fill an entire lesson or episode of learning.

In line with this idea, students could be asked to submit their plan for feedback or grading (or both) rather than having a single overall project deadline. This approach will probably also help with time (and stress) management – there is much less chance that learners will leave everything to the last minute and become overwhelmed. (See Chapter 10 for more on setting interim project deadlines.)

If this seems like babying our learners, then it's worth considering that a very similar process happens at the very highest level of academia and in the workplace. PhD students don't just start their thesis; they submit a proposal – a plan, in effect – and then get extensive feedback on this. Similar processes happen in many careers – an architect, for example, doesn't just start a building project, but first submits a bid (usually after extensive feedback from colleagues). In short, *planning as the task* is a huge part of many careers and not something to shy away from with our students.

Another area where *planning as the task* could be applied is in preparation for exam answers. We often assume that students will take a few minutes at the start of an exam or assessment to plan their answer. But do they? And if they do, do they know how to do it best, and how much time to allocate to this, so that it is impactful but doesn't eat into their writing time too much?

It's worth considering how we scaffold this, trying to make sure that students actually know what they should do – another use of the *thoughtful structure* strategy. As well as giving some guidance and structure to how long to plan for, treating planning as a separate task will help to focus students' attention on the techniques of planning, so that the bulk of their attention is not on the completion of the main task. It needn't take an entire lesson, either; as they get more confident, the writing of a quick 5-minute plan could be added into a longer lesson or done in a moment's down time. (I've observed students spending longer than that packing their bags before leaving the classroom!)

Concluding Comments

The points above outline a set of strategies that can be used to bring more of a metacognitive focus to the planning stage of a task, at times treating this like its own stand-alone task. Together, these strategies will bring more focus and a clear purpose to this phase of the learning.

Next, we will move on to the metacognitive processes that happen during the main phase of a task, taking a similar, strategy-focused approach.

Discussion Questions

What is your view of the key challenges to successful planning among your students?

Are there any ways that the planning process could be emphasised more to learners or made more transparent?

Is there a risk of helping students too much with their planning?

5 | In the Classroom, pt. 2
During the Task

The focus in this chapter will move from the *planning* to the *doing* of a classroom task. We will consider what happens during a task and identify specific metacognitive tools and strategies that can be applied.

Why Focus on Metacognition During a Task?

It might be asked why teachers would even need to focus more on metacognition during one of the main tasks of a lesson. Many of the concerns raised with respect to planning don't really apply to such tasks. Main tasks are not likely to be overlooked or have insufficient attention paid to them. Quite the opposite!

In addition, we know that working memory is limited (see Chapter 2), meaning that we should be cautious about asking students to do additional tasks or think about extra ideas.

All the same, there is certainly a risk that students are insufficiently metacognitive when they work through classroom tasks. Perhaps the biggest danger could be summarised as failing to see the wood for the trees. Students put their head down and get on with their work, failing to stop, reflect, and think about whether they are going about things correctly.

In fact, it is because of those limitations to working memory and attention, mentioned above, that problems arise (and this also explain why such issues are less likely among experts). Early in schooling, and when tackling complex new tasks, it's uncommon for students to spontaneously stop to think about strategy or reflect on their progress. For some students, there may be a persistent problem where their working memory is so occupied or indeed overloaded by a task that they lack the cognitive capacity to think about it on a metacognitive level (Gathercole, 2008). However, working memory can also be freed up through the increased automatic processing that comes with expertise, allowing schemas to be used more efficiently (Sweller et al., 2003).

Even so, this isn't the whole story – and we should be wary of simply practising the same kinds of tasks until learners can do them with ease. Learning is not just about

DOI: 10.4324/9781003386971-6

making things automatic. Gaining greater efficiency with predictable tasks has been described as *routine expertise*, but it's also important to be innovative, something known as *adaptive expertise* (Bransford et al., 2000; Hatano & Inagaki, 1986). Adaptive expertise is important for our response to novel or unpredictable tasks and therefore links to our ability to be flexibly creative, too (Gube & Lajoie, 2020).

What this shows is that it never ceases to be relevant for teachers to prompt learners to focus more on the metacognitive level as they are working on a task. Still, we should be mindful of the demands, giving learners enough time to manage the more strategy-focused aspects of their learning (e.g. by taking a 'time out' from the task itself). For more experienced classes, it can be useful to tackle overconfidence, identify misconceptions, build in variation, and push students out of their comfort zone.

If we are successful in developing students who know how to learn, then, over time, they should be able to manage this process for themselves.

Metacognitive Strategies for During the Task

Pause and Check

One of the simplest approaches to boost metacognition during a task is for teachers to make a habit of asking students to *pause and check*. This is probably happening a lot already on an ad hoc basis; teachers circulate the room to check on their learners, and if they notice something amiss, they intervene. "Why have you used that technique, Alex?" "Did you forget to round to two significant figures, Sam?"

However, in line with the argument in the previous section, learners may not (yet) be sufficiently self-regulating that they stop and think about their progress for themselves. In this context, asking students to *pause and check* can be done on a whole-class basis. It could be done routinely when they are perhaps five or ten minutes into an extended task, as you can see in Case Study 5.

Doing this regularly may help students to gain an awareness of reflection as a strategy and to see it as a useful part of the learning process, too.

> ## Case Study 5:   Analysing a Set of Data
>
> Dr R is a Business Studies teacher and has set her class the task of analysing a set of data about the UK economy. The students, all of them in their early years of secondary school, take several minutes to look at the information as Dr R circles the room, ensuring that they stay on task and that she is available to take any questions.

After around five minutes, Dr R asks students to begin planning their written answers. She directs them to plan in three sections: the key facts arising from the data, an explanation of these facts, and conclusions and implications.

Students are then directed to plan silently with pens down for a further five minutes and then to jot down points about their plan.

After this planning phase, students begin writing their answers. Many of them take a while to settle down and get into the task, but soon all are working hard, and some seem to have really gotten into the flow of the task.

It is tempting for Dr R to let the students continue, but instead she calls out to get everyone's attention and asks for pens to be put down again, with eyes on her at the front of the room.

Dr R then takes a minute to show two example pieces of writing on PowerPoint slides. She asks for comments on the piece of writing and, after a brief delay, picks a couple of students to give their views on each. One piece of writing was chosen as an example of a poorly structured response, not fitting the suggested plan, whereas the other was very accomplished. The students chosen correctly identify these issues.

The students are then set two minutes to read over what they have written so far, focusing on one question only – have they followed the plan so far?

Dr R reminds students about the three key stages of the plan, as she is aware that while they are all at different stages with their written piece, most won't have begun to work on the conclusions/implications section yet and will need a brief reminder that they should be moving on to it soon.

Finally, Dr R directs the class to continue with their silent writing.

Commentary on Case Study 5

Dr R's Business Studies lesson provides several great examples of a metacognitive approach to teaching, both in terms of planning and on the emphasis on the main task. She sets the students up well for the task, ensuring that they are not overloaded by looking at the information and writing at the same time. Her approach places an emphasis on the need to think deeply about the data, and she gives useful opportunity for questions and support/differentiation at this point.

The planning is then carefully structured into two key phases, again managing cognitive load by directing a focus on the data first and then a focus on the structure of the answer they will write. The latter structure is simple, but it is enough for students to ensure that they are covering the main aspects of what is needed. Again, the fact that a good amount of time is built in for this phase helps to ensure that students give it sufficient focus. It will lead to better results and discourage students from rushing.

The next phase of the lesson shows an example of the *pause and check* strategy. The example shows that planning is not something that happens entirely at the beginning of a process. Instead, students are constantly stopping to re-plan and think again about their next steps. Allowing time for this helps to make sure that it is successful rather than being overlooked or squeezed in terms of time. It structures and scaffolds students to do this for themselves. Perhaps at times, during other lessons, Dr R will explain to students why they are doing this, raising their awareness of strategies.

Dr R keeps things fairly simple for students by asking them to think about their own written pieces so far in comparison to the examples they have just looked at. She also shows an awareness of forgetting by reminding students about the last part of the written piece before they move on.

It may seem that Dr R's approach to guiding student writing is very controlling. However, it's likely to be more effective than having students write a piece without intervention and then giving them feedback. The metacognitive prompt will keep them on track. The more experienced students may begin to *pause and check* spontaneously.

In addition, the task doesn't require very much preparation, besides her general competence as a Business Studies teacher, her knowledge of economics, and her awareness of the course or curriculum requirements. The only materials that needed to be prepared in advance were two excepts from example answers to show on the screen – easy for a teacher to source based on previous classes' work.

Metacognitive Strategies for During the Task, Cont'd

Embracing Errors

As was briefly mentioned in Chapter 3, pre-testing (or 'pre-instruction testing') is an effective learning strategy (Richland et al., 2009). It's also a counterintuitive one. Most teachers wouldn't think to ask questions about a topic before teaching it (Pan et al., 2020). That should come later, right?

In the past, there was a popular assumption that student mistakes would become habitual and that therefore errors should be avoided (e.g. Ausubel, 1968). However, this 'errorless learning' advice conflicts with the benefits of questioning students in advance of material and the potential of learning from errors more broadly (Metcalfe, 2017). It is, in fact, good for learners to make mistakes – it connects to the desirable difficulties discussed in Chapter 2 – and can be prompted by asking students questions before they have studied the material. This is the basis of the *embracing errors* strategy.

Rather than mistakes persisting, learning by correcting a previous error appears to be highly memorable. This is known as the hypercorrection effect (see Metcalfe, 2017) and is a good example of why we need to sometimes challenge learners and push them out of their comfort zone. What's more, guessing and being incorrect does not have a harmful effect even if feedback is delayed (Kang et al., 2011).

There is also evidence that asking students to deliberately make an error can improve learning. The so-called 'derring effect' (i.e. deliberate erring) involves asking for wrong answers to a problem or incorrect examples of a concept. Wong and Lim (2022) found that deliberately generating such errors, even when students knew the right answer, led to better learning than either errorless copying or generating correct answers. This effect may derive from learners having to think about answers more deeply – not just what is right, but *why* one answer is right and another wrong (see Task 5.1).

Task 5.1

Think of a way that you could apply pre-testing or the derring effect in a class or session that you will teach soon. Try to be specific about the activity and the phase of the lesson where this can happen. Would you have considered these strategies prior to reading this chapter?

Now, take a few notes on other ways that errors might be embraced in your class and what you could do to raise awareness of this being a useful process.

Desirable difficulties such as spacing and retrieval practice (see Chapter 2) also cause more errors compared to immediate practice or copying from a slide, and so using these is another way of *embracing errors*. In total, that makes three helpful ways that students can generate errors during a task. However, as the teacher, you may need to prepare students for this as a norm and raise awareness of why it is helpful (see the 'Metacognitive Norms' section in Chapter 3).

Tackling Assumptions

As discussed earlier in this book, prior knowledge is important to learning, and what a student knows can benefit how they perform on a later task – but only if they see the relevance.

A potential hurdle to this process is that prior knowledge can be misleading, and the *tackling assumptions* strategy targets this issue. Students can experience what is known as negative transfer – they transfer ideas from one context to another when it's not relevant or helpful to do so. For example:

- Language learners may assume that grammar and vocabulary in the target language are similar to those in their native language (such as by assuming that *simpático* in Spanish means exactly the same as *sympathetic* in English);
- Students who are new to Biology may assume that soil is a plant's food and chlorophyll is the plant's blood. Here, transfer from their knowledge of people and animals is occurring (Mestre, 1994);

- Science learners may also see new terminology and confuse it with previously learned words that are superficially similar (e.g. *meiosis* and *mitosis*; Shore et al., 2015).

Tackling assumptions can be incorporated into starter tasks (along with activating prior knowledge – see Chapter 4) or later. The point is to tackle misconceptions directly, and ideally these will be discussed openly, so that everyone in the class benefits. Experienced teachers come to anticipate flawed understandings and look out for these. Ways to draw attention to and tackle such errors include the following:

- Asking critical questions. In the case of plants (see above), is there any reason to suppose that they consume food and have blood in a similar way to humans? Do they, for example, have stomachs?
- Consider other cases. If we made a flawed assumption today, could this happen again in future? Have we ever made any similar flawed assumptions in the past? This helps students to recognise a common process (see also 'Key Comparisons' section below).

Rather like the points above about errors (see *embracing errors*), it's not always a bad thing for students to have misconceptions that we later correct. It is, in any case, inevitable, but some misconceptions may return, and they need to be tackled again!

Into Words

In Chapter 3, we considered the *thinking aloud* strategy for sharing metacognitive thinking. It's also valuable for students to put their thinking *into words*.

Clearly, you can't have an entire class thinking aloud during a task, so putting student thinking *into words* is a little different and could take several formats. One option is for students to be paired up and to each explain their progress and/or strategy to a partner. This process will make them more aware of their own and each other's thinking (boosting metacognitive monitoring) and will help to clarify areas of confusion.

A silent version of the *into words* strategy would be to ask students to pause and write a short paragraph explaining how they are tackling the problem at hand or even a single sentence on a Post-it note or digital equivalent (a similar example was given in the *think-pair-share-care* strategy; see Chapter 3). Responses could be checked by a teacher as they proceed with the task. The strategy could also be built into homework tasks.

Different Ways

A central aspect of metacognition relates to students' ability to make choices about what technique to use. Regardless of the learning task, they will need to decide how they are going to tackle the task. A great way to help students to become more aware of this process is to explicitly ask them to try a different strategy or strategies – *different ways*.

Sometimes, the *different ways* strategy can be used early in a task. A student writing a persuasive essay might try several starting sentences, weighing up which is the most effective.

Alternatively, *different ways* might involve asking students to do things differently from the norm (or from what they did last time). In a cooking class, they may be asked to try *different ways* of measuring ingredients (or not doing so at all) or to try frying instead of baking and compare the outcome. When giving a presentation, students could be asked to say the same information with a different level of formality, use simpler vocabulary that a young audience could understand, or form the ideas into a story or narrative. These options help raise metacognitive awareness of the choices that can be made. If done in the same session, they may also help to directly contrast the effects of these choices.

In some cases, *different ways* could be tried immediately after completion of a piece of work. For example, with a maths problem, students could be asked to get the same result via a different method as a way of checking their work. In this and other cases, it may help if you emphasise that the purpose of the task is not just to complete/solve it but also to understand it.

There are many other examples of *different ways* to complete a task. To illustrate just a few:

- A sports team could be encouraged to switch up their positioning when making an attack.
- An art student could be encouraged to sketch in charcoal instead of pencil.
- A physics student might be encouraged to draw a scale diagram, rather than use an algebraic solution, to solve a vector problem.
- If creative writing students tend to always write rhyming poetry, encourage them to craft a poem in free verse.
- A social science student could be asked to create an infographic, rather than a standard report, to share research findings.
- If a student of a modern language always uses self-testing to study lists of vocabulary words, they could be encouraged to write them into sentences instead.

As well as being helpful for metacognitive control variation is beneficial for learning – varying our practice is a desirable difficulty (see Chapter 2). The *different ways* technique is therefore a real win-win: it boosts metacognition at the same time as supporting learning. It's easy to do, with fairly little preparation or advance planning involved. And as the final example above (modern language vocabulary) shows, students can vary their *metacognitive* strategies as well as everyday (cognitive) techniques in the classroom, such as when selecting among possible study skills (as long as they choose from options that all fit with evidence and theory – see Chapter 9 for guidance on presenting a 'menu' of suitable choices).

To further boost metacognition, you could follow up your use of this strategy with a plenary discussion of *why* different techniques might be used (or not) and what this might mean for their planning process. Highlight the fact that most learners tend to stick to a familiar approach. Nobody really likes to leave their comfort zone; this even applies to successful students at university (Bjork & Bjork, 2023). However, experts are highly flexible in how they approach a task and have a range of techniques readily at their disposal (Bransford et al., 2000). This expertise develops only if we are willing to step out of the comfort zone.

Powerful Questions

Chapter 3 discussed the benefits of supporting metacognitive talk via *scaffolded stems*, and this can be built into curriculum tasks too. By setting *powerful questions*, we can scaffold students' thinking, reflection, and problem-solving on key issues. For example, when analysing a historical story or a set of sources, students could be given a simple set of questions to answer, such as the following:

- What is the author's viewpoint?
- Who are the intended audience?
- Could the information be influenced by how the author wanted to be perceived?
- Was the author emphasising some ideas and downplaying others?

Powerful questions are widely used in some social science classrooms, but it's useful to consider that this is a way of scaffolding metacognition. Students are being guided to think about thinking – about viewpoints, multiple perspectives, and sources of bias. This is a great way to start thinking about their own perspective and (potential) biases, too. The nature of the questions may depend on the curriculum area:

- In science, questions focusing on the scientific method and possible sources of error could be the focus.
- In preparation for a debate, students could analyse the weaknesses of potential evidence and arguments they might encounter.
- For Art, Engineering, or design-focused subjects, the emphasis might be on potential pitfalls of a technique.

Depending on the group of students and their experience, you will want to consider the balance between providing *powerful questions* and having them create their own. To assist attention and memory, students could be set the task of retrieving questions from memory at any point (e.g. as a lesson starter), thus activating a relevant schema. It could also be useful to brainstorm *powerful questions* after first reading a text or pause to do so at any point during the task.

Over time, we want students to come up with similar questions for themselves spontaneously and relatively automatically, and as with other strategies, support can be withdrawn gradually, though reminders and prompts may still be needed.

Key Comparisons

The key comparisons technique aims to focus learners' attention on commonalities and differences. Comparisons can boost transfer and encourage students to think about their own learning metacognitively: "Appropriately arranged contrasts can help people notice new features that previously escaped their attention and learn which features are relevant or irrelevant to a particular concept" (Bransford et al., 2000, p. 60).

Research evidence has shown that direct comparisons can be very powerful for students' thinking. A technique called interleaving involves mixing up the order of examples or tasks, putting contrasting cases side by side. Evidence suggests that this is more effective than studying from a block of similar items, probably because of the contrasts and comparisons that it allows (see Firth, 2023, for a full discussion of interleaving in the classroom). Comparing things directly can also help students to see the similarities among two or more cases (Bauernschmidt, 2017; Carvalho & Goldstone, 2014; Gick & Holyoak, 1983), thus helping them to perceive a deeper pattern.

In a classic research study, Mary Gick and Keith Holyoak presented a set of problems to learners where the solution could be found by drawing an analogy between one problem and another. Specifically, they were told about a medical problem where doctors needed to aim lasers at a tumour to destroy it. However, a single laser was too powerful and would injure the patient. The learners had to come up with a solution that involved firing several lasers from different angles, all converging at the point of the tumour.

Some of Gick and Holyoak's learners had previously encountered an analogous problem, where a general had to march armies towards a castle, but each road was too narrow for the whole army. The solution was to divide the troops into smaller columns and approach from multiple directions. The researchers described the similarity as a 'convergence schema', where the goal was to use force to overcome a central target, and the constraint was the inability to apply full force along one path (Gick & Holyoak, 1983, p. 7). However, most participants failed to notice the correspondence; just 10% did so spontaneously, and even if instructed to memorise the first problem before trying the second, this rose only to 30%.

This shows the value in *key comparisons*. Directly hinting to students that the first problem might be useful to solve the second increased solve rates to 75%. Having students alternate between the two stories, actively looking for similarities, or providing an additional (third) story based on the same convergence schema could also help. Without these strategies that draw attention to the structure of a problem or process, students will tend to focus on surface features (Gick & Holyoak, 1983).

It is highly advantageous for students to recognise problems on a schema level (also called the deep structure of a problem) because it helps them to transfer what they have learned to new problems (Bransford et al., 2000; Gick & Holyoak, 1983). This could be applied to problem-like tasks in subjects such as English or Business Studies. Otherwise, students can become good at repeating the same set of procedures but struggle with novel formulations of problems, even when the underlying schema is the same.

There are many other ways of applying *key comparisons*. The details of the strategy may differ across different curriculum areas and might feature small-group discussion of comparisons, visual cues, demonstrations by the teacher or a peer, reading summaries that mention contrasting options, and so forth.

Waving, Not Drowning

Researchers have rightly raised concerns about the accuracy of self-assessment in education. Popular strategies such as traffic lights or a 'thumbs up' are widely used as formative assessment to indicate progress, but as discussed in Chapters 1 and 2, students' judgements of their own learning and memories are limited in terms of accuracy. Research has shown that judged performance correlates only moderately with actual success (León et al., 2023). Even a plenary quiz may indicate only what students can do at the end of the lesson (performance) rather than what they will retain over the long term (see Chapter 2).

All the same, it is good to prompt students to think about progress as they are doing a task, and you don't always want students to stop working to do so. One simple way is to ask them to give a wave to the teacher (or a thumbs up or any other gesture) as you are walking around. This *waving, not drowning* strategy is helpful because it encourages metacognitive monitoring without having to stop the task. With a wave, the student indicates to the teacher that they are fully focused, making progress, and don't want to be disturbed.

Waving, not drowning therefore provides you with the opportunity to prompt metacognitive monitoring simply by walking close to your students! Circulating around the room could be entirely silent yet still give the teacher an indication of how students are getting on. If they don't wave, it could be an indication that they are struggling ('drowning') with the task.

If you are concerned that waving might unhelpfully occupy students' working memory, consider that visuo-spatial working memory is a separate sub-store from the verbal working memory on which most schoolwork depends heavily and that multi-tasking is much easier when different modalities are used (Baddeley, 2003). Also, in line with what was said about automaticity earlier in this chapter, such a strategy will become much easier and less demanding as it becomes embedded.

Concluding Comments

The strategies described above all involve focusing on strategy during the task (e.g. by pausing to re-consider strategy) or metacognitive monitoring of the learning processes themselves. These things are effortful for students and frequently avoided. The strategies above are designed to help manage this, prompting students where necessary. Over time, all of the strategies and the metacognition involved will start to feel easier.

We have now explored metacognitive tools linked to two of the three key phases of classroom tasks – the thinking and planning before a task and the thinking that happens as it is ongoing. The third, reflection after a task, will be the focus on the next chapter.

Discussion Questions

In your experience, what are the key metacognitive problems that students face during classroom tasks? For example, do your students fail to pause and think about strategy, or are they too dependent on the teacher? Or something else?

In your view, what are the pros and cons of asking students to pause and reflect?

In the Classroom, pt. 3
After the Task

Over the past two chapters, we have focused on what happens before a task (planning and preparation) and during the work of the task itself. This chapter will continue this theme, with an emphasis now on what happens *after* the main task itself has been completed. In particular, we will explore the potential and the pitfalls involved in reflecting on learning.

Reflection is worthy of special consideration and careful thought, given that it has such a central place in the metacognition literature and is seen as a key aspect of teacher professional learning, too. Indeed, you will no doubt be aware that there is considerable emphasis on reflection across education. Many treat being a reflective learner (or a reflective practitioner) as being almost synonymous with being a *good* learner.

However, the metacognition research literature also provides reasons for caution – reasons to suppose that learners are not necessarily very good at reflecting on their own learning, even when prompted to do so. Before getting into the specifics of classroom tasks, it is worth briefly reviewing what some of this evidence shows. This will set the context for strategies that aim to overcome these limitations.

Biases, Illusions, and Myths

A key reason to anticipate that learners may not be able to reflect well on their learning comes from the psychology of biases and illusions. While everyone engages in cognition on a daily basis, this doesn't mean that we always understand or have insight into what we do and why we do it. There are a great range of biases, illusions, and myths that have been identified in psychology, each showing different ways in which most people don't understand their own minds.

Early psychologists such as Sigmund Freud recognised that people often lacked insight into their own thoughts and actions, with much of it hidden from conscious awareness. More recently, researchers in cognitive psychology have determined that our thinking is often biased, with thoughts and memory open to distortion. In their seminal work, Tversky and Kahneman (1974) showed that humans decisions and judgements are much

DOI: 10.4324/9781003386971-7

less rational than was previously assumed. For example, responses to a question about how common something is can easily be distorted by trivial factors such as how easy it is to think of an example (see Case Study 6 below).

George Miller observed that we are aware of only the *outcome* of remembering, not the process of how we achieved it (Miller, 1962). And in the legal field, the work of Elizabeth Loftus helped to show that eyewitnesses to crimes often show errors and distortions in their memories of events and, critically, are quite unaware of where they are going wrong. At a later point, people seem to be almost incapable of distinguishing the true memory from conflicting information which they encountered later (Wells & Loftus, 2013).

To focus more specifically on education, we have already seen that people typically misjudge how well they have learned, mistaking performance for learning (see Chapter 2). Here are some metacognitive illusions that have been widely documented:

The Dunning-Kruger Effect

This is the idea that people may be too ignorant of a particular issue to recognise their own ignorance. More broadly, this means that learners (especially novices) may overestimate their own competence, misjudge how well they have mastered a task or skill or area of expertise, and lack any awareness of what they are missing.

The Lake Wobegon Effect

This effect, named after a fictional town created by American author Garrison Keillor, is where people experience illusory superiority in their skills compared to the average. Research has found a large majority of people believing themselves to be above average in attributes like social charisma, driving, and leadership skills. In reality, only half of us can be above average!

The Fundamental Attribution Error

This is where people overestimate the role of the situation and circumstances when it comes to their own behaviour and underestimate the role of personality and abilities. This is reversed when thinking about other people – a tendency to assume that their behaviour is due to their (relatively fixed) traits such as their personality or talent. For example, if we see a classmate cursing and getting annoyed, we might think that this is because they are a disagreeable person. If we ourselves curse and get annoyed, we are more likely to attribute this to being tired or to the task we are working on being exceptionally hard.

The Planning Fallacy

This effect relates to how much time people allocate to their work. Most people underestimate the time it will take to do a task, and their estimates of when they will finish tend to be highly over-optimistic. The effect persists even when learners are provided with plenty of information about how long such tasks typically take for comparison groups of similar people.

The Learning Styles Myth

This is one of a range of learning myths (often called 'neuromyths') that involve categorising ourselves. Most people (students and teachers alike) incorrectly believe that learners can be grouped into simplistic categories such as 'visual learners' and 'kinaesthetic learners'. In reality, there is no evidence that grouping learners in this way or trying to cater for their supposed learning style makes any difference to attainment (Pashler et al., 2008) or even that such styles exist. Inaccurate labelling may well cause a student harm due to unhelpful constraints, perhaps by having them believe that they won't benefit from reading or from using visual diagrams. There are various learning styles theories, but all have the same underlying problems (An & Carr, 2017; see also Chapter 12). Now, it is worth saying that there is often more nuance in the research than can be communicated in the simple summaries above. In some cases, there are contrary results in the research literature, with biases disappearing under certain circumstances. In others, the phenomena haven't been thoroughly tested outside of the Western, well-educated populations that psychologists tend to study (see Henrich et al., 2010) or with younger learners.

Nevertheless, the sheer number of findings across a range of domains and situations do send a clear message that human psychology in general is often not intuitive. People lack clear insight into how their own mental processes work, and do not carry with them an instruction book for their own mind (Pan & Bjork, 2021). And even our own knowledge (the content of long-term memory) is only partially accessible to us. It seems clear that metacognition is prone to inaccuracies, even if we are not *always* inaccurate.

Beliefs about the Self

In addition, besides specific and well-documented myths, learners may hold a range of inaccurate beliefs about themselves, such as believing that they are not creative, that their brain can't do maths, that they can't work well in the morning, and so forth. This self-labelling can be highly self-limiting and overlaps with the concept of having a fixed mindset (see Chapter 11 for more on that).

Reflection and Memory

Bear in mind also that long-term memory is prone to rapid forgetting and distortion (see Chapter 2). Learners may not accurately remember the classroom events that they are supposed to be reflecting on! In the absence of solid, verifiable information, they instead make inferences on the basis of incidental events (e.g. how quickly they finished) or subjective feelings (did it feel like I understood?) when reflecting on past experiences (Sanna & Schwarz, 2007).

In this context, we should be wary about assuming that our students will reflect accurately on their thinking or learning. It is worth emphasising that all of the above metacognitive illusions connect to fundamental ideas summarised in Chapters 1 and 2. If students don't understand their own cognition, then their metacognitive judgements are likely to be flawed as well (Kornell & Bjork, 2007).

Judging the Accuracy of Reflection

One of the most commonly used approaches in metacognition research is to compare estimates of learning with actual learning. This allows us to measure the calibration between estimate and reality.

For example, we could set a class a test on which students would gain a percentage score, and then – before they received their grade – ask them to estimate the grade they would get. A teacher or researcher could quickly and easily look for a correlation between the two (a high correlation suggests that estimates are generally accurate) or other patterns.

This body of research has suggested that estimates are often rather inaccurate but that there are some circumstances that can increase the accuracy of reflections – or make them worse.

Estimates appear to be biased by ease and fluency, meaning that learners will overestimate their performance on a task that felt easy. In some cases, they will judge a less effective study strategy to be superior due to this bias (e.g. Kornell & Bjork, 2008; Yan et al., 2017). Learners often judge their understanding to be better than it actually is, too, due to factors such as how quick and easy it was to read a text (Singer Trakhman et al., 2023).

Overall, learners' self-assessment of their own performance can be flawed, but we can begin to tackle this via the basic metacognitive practices outlined earlier in this book (e.g. see Chapter 3), such as *thinking aloud* and *misconceptions corner*. These raise students' general awareness of metacognitive processes. We will now look at further, targeted ways to improve student reflection. These are the focus of the next section.

Reflective Strategies

Let's now move on to some recommended strategies. Perhaps you will notice how these are carefully chosen to tackle the points that have been raised in the chapter so far (see Task 6.1).

> ## Task 6.1
>
> As you work through the strategies in the next section, take note of any illusions or biases to which they link. Can you see how the strategies have been chosen to tackle these?

Mastering Mistakes

Building on the idea of *thinking aloud* (see Chapter 3), teachers can provide useful role models at various points in a lesson, and one is how they react to mistakes. When students see a teacher respond to an error, it provides a model that they can draw on when reflecting for themselves, such as when they gain a bad grade.

A teacher can be a superb role model in terms of how to react to mistakes. Students may be embarrassed about their own errors and may clam up rather than wanting to talk about them. The teacher can show not only that is it fine to talk about errors but that these can be very informative.

With the *mastering mistakes* strategy, the focus is on modelling how you would work out where an error came from. Was it inattention to some aspect of the problem? In discussing this, you are discussing your own thinking and raising awareness of some of the limitations of cognition (e.g. that it's easy to overlook minor details or make mistakes through habit).

The onus then shifts onto the students to master their own mistakes and to demonstrate this to the teacher or to peers. Sharing their own mistakes and explaining why they made them could be set up as a group task.

Many teachers feel understandably wary about displaying their own fallibility to a class. All the same, it is important for students to see that you are a human being who can make mistakes, and it will probably make you more relatable, too! Further, the process of your response acts as an important think-aloud, demonstrating the process of reflecting and responding to surprising or unwanted outcomes.

Some aspects of the *mastering mistakes* strategy might include the following:

- Looking for specific reasons. A successfully metacognitive learner will avoid general statements along the lines of "I'm bad at this topic" and instead try to pinpoint the exact issue that led to them losing marks. Specific feedback is more helpful for improvement (Ericsson, 2017), and a teacher can model the process of identifying *exactly* what they did wrong;

- A healthy emotional response. It's easy to feel embarrassed about mistakes, but the teacher can show students a different approach – amusement or curiosity about errors, perhaps. Being mildly frustrated is fine as well, as it provides a healthy alternative to catastrophising;

- Dwelling on the issue. Connected to their emotional response, students may want to rush past an error and think about it as little as possible. The teacher can demonstrate that it's worthwhile to pause and get to the bottom of a mistake, to dwell on it, and to treat it as a fun puzzle to be solved.

Bear in mind that this strategy doesn't need to end with the awareness of identifying mistakes or modelling a response. Giving students time to tackle and correct mistakes for themselves is also important! And as their confidence grows, students could be asked to both find and correct mistakes in sample work.

Five-Minute Judgements

A quick and dirty approach to reflection after a task is to ask students for a simplistic overall letter grade, percentage, or 'traffic light' (red, amber, or green) to indicate how students thought that they got on.

Many teachers will ask students, "How did you get on with that? Was it easy or hard?" Fewer may ask, "What percentage do you think you got?", though the latter question has the advantage that this can then be compared with their actual performance after the work has been checked or graded, as discussed earlier. This approach can help to reveal instances where your students' judgements are inaccurate.

The latter approach can be extended by asking students to take a few minutes to explain why they believe they got a particular grade, perhaps writing a paragraph or a set of bullet points in their notebooks. A timer could be set for five minutes for them to both give their estimate and justify it in writing. Hopefully, in most cases, you will see a gradual improvement in the calibration between student estimates and actual outcomes, though it can be interesting (and metacognitively enlightening) to see how much harder this is with an unfamiliar type of task or assessment.

Delayed Reflection

One strategy that is already widely used in education, and that prompts an element of metacognitive thinking, is to ask students what they learned today. This could take the form of looking back at learning objectives, an 'exit pass' (a slip of paper where students answer a few questions before leaving the class – not to be confused with a toilet pass!), or some other way of asking students to consider what they think they've learned before the end of a lesson.

Again, though, this strategy is subject to metacognitive illusions. Students are poor at summarising what they have learned and may miss key points. In addition, responses on an exit pass may reflect performance rather than learning. Connecting back to the previous strategy, the ease of recalling something immediately (or soon) after studying it may bias them towards thinking that they know it better than they actually do. This is where *delayed reflection* comes in.

It has been found that a brief delay to judgements of learning can make them more accurate. You may recall the study by Koriat and Bjork (2005) which was described in Chapter 2. This found that even a ten-minute delay was sufficient to greatly increase students' accuracy – they were better able to judge their own forgetting.

Therefore, teachers could consider waiting until after a break or interval before asking for such reflections, thereby prompting *delayed reflection*. If this isn't practical (e.g. because you teach only one short lesson), consider asking for reflection at the beginning of the next class instead. The answers are likely to be much more informative to you as a teacher, and they are less likely to mislead students into a false sense of confidence. (The *pop quizzes* strategy described in Chapter 3 also implies reflection after a delay.)

Prove It

As already discussed, students may incorrectly overestimate what they know or can do, a bias that reflects their focus on performance rather than learning. Recently studied ideas will sound familiar to them, leading to overconfidence in judging their own knowledge or skills.

A remedy to this recommended by Robertson (2021) is to add a further *prove it* section to reflections on how strong students feel at a particular task. For example, if a student were asked to rate their understanding of the work of Pablo Picasso, they wouldn't just tick a box or fill in a smiley face – they would have to list one or more facts to exemplify what they know.

The *prove it* strategy could be extended further (and made even more metacognitive) by asking them to list an area where they have recently improved their knowledge or overcome a misconception. And you might notice that, in many cases, having to *prove it* will act as a form of retrieval practice as well. Another win-win for metacognition!

Activating Feedback

Students get a lot of feedback in school, and much of it is largely ignored because it is unwelcome (Wiliam, 2011) – students simply don't want to hear it. The feedback may be good quality, but it isn't doing much to help the learning process.

This may connect in part with students' attitudes to and beliefs about learning – and about themselves. If students believe that their performance is a sign of their ability (e.g. "I'm not good at maths"), then a grade of 55% may just be par for the course rather than stimulating them to take action (though hopefully you have been demonstrating a different approach via *mastering mistakes* – see above!).

To tackle this, it is important to frame feedback in terms of improvements and to make these as specific and concrete as possible. What are the next steps, how do learners take them, and where do the priorities lie? What should they do if they need to find out more? These are often the priorities for feedback. Consider the following examples:

- "In future, your essays need to be more richly described."
- "In future, ensure that you provide examples of concepts such as 'injustice'."

I think you'll agree that the second example of feedback is more specific, directing the student to what they need to change in their writing in a way that will make sense to them and that most students could actually act upon.

Remember, students get an easy 'out' if they are allowed to move on without acting on this feedback. Instead, you might wish to have them engage in *extended plans* (see Chapter 3) by planning an improved response or to try *mastering mistakes* by re-writing flawed answers.

Zombie Feedback

At times, it may feel to students that their feedback is like a zombie in a TV show – it just keeps returning even when you think you've dealt with it!

Are they constantly being told that they were careless with their working, that they are misusing apostrophes, or that their shading in art is sloppy? Understandably, they may get sick of hearing the same message after a while. However, this motivation can be useful for the teacher. You can ask them to explain and justify why they no longer need the feedback. In short, it's up to them to kill off that zombie for good.

Perhaps the student could say how their original piece of work didn't (in their view) fully reflect their skills. Or they could make a case that the feedback didn't entirely capture some aspects of the work. Such a defence could be done during a one-to-one discussion, or they could be asked to make a written comment in response to feedback on a task.

The value of such reflections on feedback is that they are inherently metacognitive. The task forces students to think deeply about their own learning process, to reflect, and to form an argument about their skill or knowledge. In doing so, they can (perhaps) show you that they are ready to progress without the zombie feedback; you can reward them by finally consigning it to its eternal grave.

Case Study 6:   Subject Choices

Mrs Jones is a Music teacher and is speaking to Kim, a student in the early stages of secondary school who is just about to make her subject choices for next year. The choices Kim makes now will affect her for the next few years of school at least and could also affect her future university or career plans.

81

> Mrs Jones knows for sure that Kim has really enjoyed many of the things that she has studied in Music over the past year. Even when the work was hard and technical, she appeared to find it rewarding. She also commented several times on how important she considers it to engage with the cultural side of learning and showed a real flair for creative ideas in the music technology part of her course (e.g. in her sound engineering work). It's clear that she has found it enriching.
>
> However, Kim got a poorer-than-usual grade on her latest test and has been dwelling on this when considering her subject choices. She has also commented that she'd rather work towards a better-paid career, for example in science or business.
>
> Mrs Jones feels disappointed that Kim is not considering her earlier experiences and successes and that she appears to be drawing on a negative stereotype of music careers that springs easily to mind.

Comment on Case Study 6

The frustrations that Mrs Jones feels about Kim's subject choices will be familiar to many teachers and to parents as well. Often, students don't seem to make the best choices and are swayed by rather temporary situations rather than taking all factors into account.

In particular, the case study shows how much focus a student can put on a test score. This is highly salient by being recent and fresh in their mind. Previous experiences, however valuable at the time, are easily pushed aside. This links to the cognitive biases discussed earlier in this chapter. The next and final strategy in this chapter – *Looking forward* – is highly relevant to the situation.

Reflective Strategies, Cont'd

Looking Forward

A key aspect of the reflection process is to look forward and make decisions about the future. However, in line with the illusions and biases discussed earlier, it can be assumed that decision making about future work and study will often be suboptimal! Case study 6 provided a good example of the problems this can cause.

People's thinking about the future can be biased in various ways. As mentioned earlier, judgements can be biased by how easy it is to think of information (Tversky & Kahneman, 1974). People may make decisions based on the readily available information rather than considering the broader picture. This is known as *the availability heuristic*. It can lead to information that is fresh in our mind (such as recently heard opinions or today's test scores) drowning out more important ideas.

To tackle this issue, we need to equip students with strategies for looking forward in a less biased way. We can make other information more salient by having learners keep a *looking forward* record that they can refer back to. This will include reflections throughout the year or course and may feature comments on things they found interesting or valuable.

When making a decision with such a record in front of them, students are less likely to be biased by recent information, as other points become much more obvious and salient (though, of course, some may become out of date). It results in their behaviour and choices being 'nudged' in helpful ways, by making certain things more memorable, appealing, or easier (Sunstein, 2014).

People are also highly motivated to maintain consistency in their behaviour (Cialdini et al., 2002; Festinger, 1954). They tend to stick to their declared interests or aspirations (especially if they have shared these publicly). This is another way that a *looking forward* record acts as a nudge to stick to those same goals.

Reflection and Time

A general issue relevant to many of the strategies and situations discussed in this chapter so far is that it often takes a long time to get feedback in education. A test score may arrive days or weeks after a student studies for the test, whereas exam grades are received months or even years after their work on a course begins. This makes effective reflection on our learning quite challenging.

Often, learners will be reflecting on their work or their understanding before they have had a chance to get feedback from an expert, and they may need to take important decisions (such as what subject to take, as in Case Study 6) prior to getting their exam results.

As Hogarth et al. (2015) discuss, we can characterise some learning situations as 'wicked learning environments' – ones where there is a mismatch between feedback and later applications, or the potential use of feedback is otherwise hindered or obscured. This is further complicated by issues such as performance vs. learning, forgetting, flawed inferences based on incidental events (e.g. how quickly they finished), and subjective feelings (did it *feel* like I understood?), as discussed earlier in this chapter.

In this sense, many educational settings are very different from throwing a dart or playing a chord on a piano, because in those circumstances, a mistake is (usually) immediately obvious. It also contrasts with the optimal conditions for developing expertise. Some of the most effective ways of promoting learning across many domains, from sport to music to professional learning, are associated with practice that gains rapid, specific feedback (Ericsson, 2017). In these, the learner gets this feedback from either an expert or the task outcome itself, facilitating a 'deliberate practice' approach (see Ericsson, 2017).

While some settings in education (sports, music, etc.) can at least use elements of this approach, many academic education settings will struggle to make feedback as quick and clear as would be ideal.

However, there are things that we can do. The problem of ineffective feedback is one of the motivations behind calls to make learning more 'visible' (e.g. Hattie & Clarke, 2018), meaning that learners and teachers alike should know when learning is happening and when it is not. This idea is very concordant with a metacognitive approach to teaching. Indeed, many of the strategies throughout this book have been about making learning processes and their outcomes clearer to the learner:

- into words;
- pop quizzes;
- delayed reflection;
- and many more!

The wickedness of the learning environment depends in part on the learner's assumptions and biases (Hogarth et al., 2015). A metacognitive approach to teaching – and to reflection – can make it just that bit kinder for our students.

Task 6.2

Bearing in mind the points made about reflection and timing, is there anything you can do in your context to make feedback quicker, more salient, or more specific? Try to make a list. If you are struggling with this, discuss it with a small group of colleagues and share your ideas.

On Teachers' Reflection

The points throughout this chapter have indicated that students' ability to reflect accurately can't be taken for granted. However, neither can that of teachers! Despite the expectation of teachers to be reflective practitioners, many of the same points are likely to apply to teachers' judgement of their own learning, too. Consider, for example:

- What you learned from a recent professional talk or course;
- What you are learning from a book like this;
- How you retain factual information about your teaching subject.

Even experts are likely subject to many of the same metacognitive biases discussed so far in this section. So why not try out some of the same strategies to tackle them?

Task 6.3

Draw a table with two columns in your notes. Make a quick list in the left column to show biases and other problems that you can recall from what you've read in this chapter. In the right column, note down how they might apply to teaching. Try to do this task from memory at first and then check back through the last few pages. Leave space to add more that you encounter elsewhere.

Where in particular might inaccuracies lie? Unfortunately, all of the biases, illusions, and myths mentioned earlier in this chapter apply to adults. There is no reason to suppose that any of these is absent among teachers. From what we know about metacognition, it's probably safest to assume that our metacognition won't always be accurate.

To be optimistic, we might hope that expertise counteracts these things at least a little. But focusing on the Lake Wobegon effect for a moment, how many teachers would say they are 'above average' at what they do? You could try asking a few colleagues! A concerning bit of context here comes from Ehrlinger et al. (2008, p. 98): "poor performers grossly overestimate their performances because their incompetence deprives them of the skills needed to recognize their deficits".

It's also not hard to think of situations where feedback is problematic and obscures improvement in some way. I have certainly witnessed student teachers being given feedback such as "You need to show more presence". The lack of specificity of such guidance, while perhaps not inaccurate, makes it very hard to act on, as discussed in connection with some of the strategies above.

The feedback loop is also very slow for teachers – often even more so than for students – leading to another wicked learning environment. Without an external observer, we have no real way of objectively scoring the quality of our own explanations or questioning, for example. Teachers are also subject to imperfect memories, just like anyone else, meaning that what we remember about our own teaching may be flawed. Besides this, all we have to base our reflection on is our students' later attainment; comparison of this with previous cohorts is imperfect at best. Finally, teachers may misjudge performance for learning.

A fuller discussion of teacher reflections is beyond the scope of this book, but we will return to ideas around implementing metacognition on a whole-school level in Chapter 12 and consider the role it plays in teachers' professional knowledge. For now, the points above help us to understand that accurate reflection can't be taken for granted.

Reflecting on Learning – Concluding Comments

In this chapter, we have looked at the difficulties inherent in reflecting on learning. Despite the huge prominence given to this process throughout education, we have seen that there are many pitfalls. We have also looked at several strategies for tackling these issues in the classroom. Each of these aims to make reflections more accurate. Next up, we will focus on metacognition in the specific context of literacy.

Discussion Questions

Which of the myths and misconceptions in this chapter did you find most interesting?

Are there any of the myths and misconceptions where you'd like more information? Could you explore these independently, perhaps as a group?

Do you agree with the argument that successful reflection can't be taken for granted? If so, which strategy strikes you as the most useful way of improving it?

7 | A Metacognitive Approach to Literacy

Having considered some of the quick wins for a metacognitive classroom (Chapter 3) as well as how to weave a metacognitive approach into curriculum tasks from planning through to reflection (Chapters 4–6), we'll now focus in on a key set of skills that apply to every area of the curriculum: literacy.

For every subject area, it's vital that learners can listen well, express themselves verbally, write in accurate and well-structured ways, and read texts. So, what can metacognition offer to educators for supporting these skills in particular?

The evidence and scholarship about the teaching of writing and (especially) reading are extensive, so it should be emphasised before proceeding that this chapter is about how a metacognitive approach can help reading and writing to become more effective, rather than covering all of the ways to teach these skills in the first place. As you will see, there are many useful strategies that can enhance students' literacy, all of which mesh well with and build on what has been covered so far.

How Metacognition Connects

As we consider how metacognition connects to literacy skills, it's worth briefly circling back to an idea mentioned near the start of this book: the *cognitive level* and the *metacognitive level* of thinking (see Chapter 1).

As a brief reminder, the cognitive level includes the thinking that a student is doing as they engage in a task. Cognitive processes include thinking, paying attention, remembering, and language. All of these are fully engaged during any literacy task.

The metacognitive level, meanwhile, involves our knowledge of our cognition, monitoring it as it happens or making strategic decisions (control) for how to act. These aspects of metacognition underpin all of the strategies throughout this book; everything depends on the accuracy of a learner's knowledge and monitoring and the soundness of the strategic decisions they make. In literacy, they are apparent in processes such as thinking about the purpose or value of reading, paying attention to your written style as you

DOI: 10.4324/9781003386971-8

craft a piece of writing, or choosing a different strategy when looking for information from a text.

Because of the demands of reading as a skill, it is likely to be taking place mainly at the cognitive level for most learners. However, it can certainly be enhanced by some of the metacognitive strategies covered so far. Like any other task, reading can benefit from effective planning and reflection. You can ask learners how they intend to organise their reading (*pointful planning*) and delay questions about what they learned from it (*delayed reflection*), for example.

Metacognitive monitoring is more difficult for beginner readers, as their working memory will be fully occupied by the demanding task of understanding the words. As they become more skilful readers, the basic decoding of letters and words becomes increasingly automatic in that it requires relatively little attention. With this automaticity established, attention can more easily engage in metacognitive monitoring. They can, for example, think about the following:

- Is this text making sense to me?
- Am I finding the information that I wanted from this text?
- Am I enjoying this story?
- How does this compare to the previous text I read?

For writing, metacognition is even more intimately connected, in part because writers of all ages and levels are creating a text, not engaging with one that is already written. Even experienced writers frequently stop to think about what they are writing and where to go next. Some researchers have referred to writing as "applied metacognition" (Hacker et al., 2009, p. 154) due to how closely the skill is interwoven with the writer's strategic thinking. When a student writes a text, even a short one, they are continually thinking about what they are trying to say and how they want to say it – essential aspects of metacognition. Writing is a complex skill and one that (except, perhaps, at the most basic beginner level) depends on our capacity to thinking about thinking.

In the following two sections, we will explore metacognitive strategies which can be applied to promoting literacy. We will begin with reading, then move on to writing, and finally look at some strategies that are relevant to literacy more broadly.

Better Reading

As we tend to view reading as a skill, it's perhaps easy to underestimate the role of memory. However, every aspect of reading depends fundamentally on knowledge (broadly defined) as stored in long-term memory. Everything from the sounds and meanings of words to the shapes of letters in familiar languages must be retained. In fact, one thing that distinguishes the reader from the non-reader (or the weak reader) is how well these are stored and how easily and automatically they come to mind. A baby hasn't yet stored any of this information, whereas an illiterate adult knows word meanings but has not (fully) connected them to the shapes of letters or words.

An understanding of memory therefore links directly to learning reading, and concepts like the spacing effect and retrieval practice can be applied directly. For example, what is the best point to come back and practice phonics or whole words? These things will be subject to forgetting, and delayed (spaced) practice is likely to be more effective. Interleaving of contrasting items can boost learning too (see Chapter 5), and interleaving of easily confused spellings or letter shapes would fit well with this concept, as would interleaving of styles of writing or genre.

Reading also boosts memory, of course. This can be enhanced using some of the techniques described in the previous chapters. For example, you could use pre-testing with a text or other approaches that generate errors (the *embracing errors* strategy). Students could be encouraged to question themselves or make predictions before reading and to reflect on these afterwards. Retaining knowledge of what has been read will lead to a virtuous cycle, making future reading easier.

A Profile of Reading Sub-Skills

A metacognitive approach to learning places an emphasis on learners' perception of their own skill, and this can also be applied to reading. To achieve this, teachers may want to place a certain emphasis on helping learners to become diagnostic about their own reading. Do they know where their strengths lie and what they need to practise? Do they have a realistic appreciation of their overall profile as a reader?

It's likely that many students have a fairly inaccurate sense of their reading skills. They may judge themselves via fairly arbitrary comparisons (e.g. with a sibling or a classmate that they sit next to). The teacher may wish to guide students instead to begin recording their progress against targets (a use of the *tracked thinking* strategy; see Chapter 3). This could be done in a quite a visual way; for example, they could fill in a bar graph after each time that they practice a sub-skill such as skimming, scanning, intensive reading, or extensive reading (Krashen & Terrell, 1998).

The teacher could encourage the class not only to improve the various sub-skills of reading but also to try to get a more balanced profile (so they don't have one reading sub-skill that is much more developed than all the others).

A word of caution applied to this strategy: remember that learners are not very good at judging their own ability! Some care needs to be taken over where this information comes from. Simply asking learners to reflect on their own reading is unlikely to lead to an accurate profile, and they also shouldn't judge these sub-skills on the basis of a single task or test.

Knowledge is Power(ful)

Background knowledge is a barrier to reading for many learners; if this either is lacking in general or is incompatible with the content of the text, students will find it much harder to read (Hirsch, 2003). Any text, simple storybooks included, requires a certain level of factual knowledge to interpret. This is easily demonstrated for yourself by picking up an advanced textbook on an unfamiliar subject. You may be able to understand the words, but without knowledge of the concepts, it's very hard to understand the text as a whole.

For that reason, pre-teaching of relevant concept knowledge can be excellent preparation for reading a text at any stage and level. This can be as simple as defining a set of key terms as a starter task. You may also give an overview explanation of a concept or area or show a video before they begin to read. A more elaborate example would be engaging in an entire project or topic, preparing learners to then tackle a book on the same theme.

As well as making a text easier to read, prior knowledge helps students to retain more, as they will be able to make more links and inferences and think more deeply about its meaning. They may also form personal connections between the text and their prior learning. Deeper, meaningful, personalised thinking is more memorable (Bransford et al., 2000; Symons & Johnson, 1997).

Helping Students to Recognise Style, Purpose, and Genre

There is a great deal that we want our students to gain from a text beyond just understanding it at a basic level. When reading a novel, for example, can they recognise and discuss the unspoken messages or themes? In a persuasive piece, can they see how an effective author constructs their argument? Generally, do they find the text fun to read?

Clearly, the fundamentals of reading are prerequisite to the points above, but there are other things that we can do on a metacognitive level, including the following:

- Talking about texts you have enjoyed and why. Some students may not even realise that reading can be enlightening and/or amusing. As well as the teacher modelling this (a form of *think aloud*; see Chapter 3), peers could talk about their favourites;
- Talk about the purpose of a text, with some historical, political, or biographical background relating to when it was written;
- Don't push the learner to a high reading level too quickly. Levelling up the demands of the text makes it harder for them to appreciate it more holistically (again, working memory will be too busy with basic processes). Not only will they gain less from a text that is too hard (in comparison with an easier, diverting read), it could hinder their motivation.

Reading Widely Can Boost Skills and Knowledge

Most teachers want their students to read widely. It's certainly true that sustained practice can make a difference to reading skills and that it can impact on vocabulary, too (though usually in combination with other strategies; see Wasik et al., 2016). In line with the points about reading level in the previous section (see above), don't neglect the benefits of reading less literary sources too. Texts such as comics, fan fiction, or blogs can all form part of the mix and may be more motivating than more traditional options (and motivating the learners can be a win in itself). If you're concerned about the accuracy or quality of some such texts, perhaps that could be a learning objective in addition (See Task 7.1.)

It's also going to be helpful to tackle a range of types of material. Practice of the skills involved in reading will be more impactful if that practice is varied, because variation is a desirable difficulty. Contrasts between texts can also help students to understand on a metacognitive level how genre works (see the "Key Comparisons" section in Chapter 5).

Non-fiction texts have benefits that connect to both variation and prior knowledge. Students can develop their knowledge more directly from reading these texts than from fiction (though that also helps), potentially leading to a win-win in terms of reading practice and knowledge development. Therefore, if students are drawn to non-fiction, it can certainly be encouraged. Perhaps you can even have a metacognitive discussion about what students have learned from fiction versus non-fiction.

Task 7.1

Make a short list of the texts that learners read in your context. How many of these were written specifically for education? Are there ways that you could include less typical kinds of texts, such as comics or blogs?

Would there be room to explore contrasts between good quality and poorer texts? For example, are students learning to recognise biased sources in your subject area?

Informing Students about Automaticity

As mentioned above, many aspects of reading as a skill will become gradually more automatic with practice. On a metacognitive level, it can be valuable to raise this idea with students, especially new or struggling readers. It's important that they don't see themselves as inherently poor readers or believe that it will never get easier. In line with the key metacognitive message about learning as a skill that we have explored throughout the book, reading is very susceptible to practice. And when automated, it becomes much easier to monitor and reflect on one's reading, as mentioned earlier.

However, the automaticity of skilled readers can be a mixed blessing. At times, teachers may need to prompt the more skilled readers to stop and think about what they are reading. This is particularly true when it comes to reading non-fiction; students may need to think more strategically about such skills as scanning a text for information or evaluating their own reading process. Like other automatic cognitive processes, they lack monitoring and control unless we make an effort to build these things back in.

An understanding of automatic processes can become part of students' developing metacognitive knowledge about reading. It may be useful to ask them to think of analogies of other skills and procedures that can become partly automatic, such as getting dressed in the morning, and how this can be both useful and prone to errors.

Case Study 7:   Stumbling Over the Words

Rena is a keen reader in primary school. She has been enjoying reading storybooks in school, but sometimes she rushes and stumbles over the words. She also tends to get quite a few details wrong when asked about the stories, and she often skips several small words when reading aloud.

Her teacher, Mr W, realises that while Rena is a capable reader, there are some issues that will hold her back. He speaks to Rena and is interested to hear Rena express the view that 'a good reader is a really fast reader!' and that 'smart kids read the harder books'. Mr W gently explains to Rena that even though she's in a rush to get to the end of the story, she'll enjoy stories much more if she slows down a bit and ensures that she is reading every word. He also explains that sometimes our eyes move faster than our brains can read the words.

Mr W comes to realise that Rena's beliefs about reading are causing problems. Because she wants to be one of the smart kids, she is choosing books that are too hard. And because she is keen to get to the end, she is skipping words rather than decoding them.

Mr W speaks to an educational psychologist, and they agree that Rena should tackle some easier books for now. At first, Rena finds this frustrating because she wanted to stick with the same books, but the school librarian is able to identify suitable alternatives that cover similar topics but that are less challenging. Mr W also asks her to slow down and think if she comes to a word she doesn't know, sounding it out and trying to guess what it means.

Even when sounding out the occasional word, Rena quickly regains her previous reading speed with the easier books. She is also much more accurate at reading aloud and is no longer skipping words. Soon, Rena is ready to move on to the harder books that she chose before.

Discussion of Case Study 7

The case study shows a potential downside of automation in reading – as well as accurate reading and decoding becoming more automatic, bad habits (such as skipping difficult words) can too! Mr W was rightly concerned that Rena was struggling despite her fluency and took effective action to tackle it.

Of course, sometimes there are deeper underlying issues with reading. For example, skipping words can be a sign of dyslexia. Mr W spoke to the educational psychologist when agreeing the best strategy and drew on the expertise of the librarian for book recommendations at the right difficulty level.

The Mysteries of Writing

Writing is perhaps even more mysterious than reading. At least with reading, most young students come into school aware of the existence of books and stories. When adults read aloud to them in the early years, it provides a good insight into what the experience of reading is like.

There is a further level of mystery when it comes to writing. What exactly is it like to write a text? Until students have tried to do this for themselves, it's no doubt hard to imagine. And even when they begin writing in early primary school, the slow and ponderous nature of their beginner writing is very different from the experience of writing as a skilled adult.

It can be useful to tackle misconceptions about writing at all stages of education. Some things that students may not appreciate include the following:

- Writing can be done for pleasure or for practical communication;
- Most extended pieces of writing are planned;
- Most extended pieces of writing were extensively edited before being published;
- Writers tend to write with a particular audience in mind.

As students may carry with them a flawed metacognitive understanding of writing as a process, it's important to raise awareness that writing is complex but learnable.

Young children's writing shows key differences to that of older students. In particular, beginner writers do not plan out what they are going to write. They engage in what Bereiter and Scardamalia (1987) call a 'know-tell' process; they know something and then they write it down. Often, one idea leads to the next, with very little in the way of a plan or metacognitive overview of what they are trying to do.

As they mature, students soon become capable of planning texts more carefully. However, unless they are guided to do so (perhaps with the help of *thoughtful structure* – see Chapter 4), many may still neglect the planning stage. Some may see this as unnecessary (see above) or rush it. And if they do plan, they may not appreciate the value of reflecting on a plan or getting feedback on it.

Prior Knowledge

We have probably all experienced interruptions to our writing when we need to stop and look something up. This phenomenon shows how – just as with reading (see above) – fundamental concept knowledge can be a barrier to fluent writing.

This issue is particularly applicable to non-fiction writing (e.g. crafting discursive pieces in the social science or persuasive writing in English), though it can crop up in creative writing too. One solution links back to the planning stage – aim to guide writers to ensure that they have all (or at least most) of the information they will need before beginning.

It's better still if they have the information in their long-term memory, and working to make this more likely indicates how long we should potentially plan for a piece of writing. With time allocated to initial teaching, *pop quizzes* and other consolidation, and perhaps a further active review session ahead of the actual writing task, the chances of students being able to easily bring key facts and figures to mind are greatly increased (after which the process of writing acts as further retrieval practice).

A group discussion or *think-pair-share-care* task (see Chapter 3) could also help learners to judge their current knowledge level and helps to make schemas more accessible (Anderson, 2018).

Written Competence

Going hand in hand with factual knowledge relevant to their written piece is the student's competence with the written language itself. How often do they need to stop to look words up, check spelling, or think about grammar? To some extent, such pauses and interruptions are a normal and natural process that even educated adults experience. It's not hard to see, however, that this can be very disruptive for beginner writers and needs to be managed.

One simple metacognitive strategy is to ask learners to overlook spelling and grammar for a first draft. This could be linked to an awareness-raising discussing of the limitations of their working memory. They can come back and review spelling and grammar later, in an editing stage. This strategy can encourage learners to write more fluently and make it less of an ordeal but also highlights the fact that language errors can be thought about and reflected upon.

Written competence doesn't extend just to spelling and grammar. Students may struggle with issues such as using linking words, strategically varying the length of sentences for style and impact, paragraphing, or the formality of language used. A review of these things during the redrafting stage will help to boost their language competence ahead of future written tasks, leading to a virtuous cycle as it becomes easier for them to avoid mistakes in initial drafts.

Achieving Flow

As the building blocks of writing such as spelling and sentence construction become more automatic, it becomes easier for the writer to enter a 'flow state'. This is where their attention is fully engaged and less easily distracted, focusing entirely on the task at hand. Time may even seem to pass more quickly for the student when they are in flow, and performance can improve (Nakamura & Csikszentmihalyi, 2009).

Skill level is important to achieving flow because it depends on a match between the student's competence and the difficulty of the task. Weak writers are not likely to enter a flow state, because they struggle and get frustrated. However, as long as the task is not too complicated, even relatively young writers can enter flow.

It's worth considering that, despite its benefits, a flow state also makes it harder for a writer to monitor what they are doing, in line with the points made about automaticity earlier in this chapter. They may be engaging in bad language habits, automatic spelling errors, and so forth. As with reading, it may be useful for the teacher to periodically interrupt students when they are mid-task, particularly if you have noticed students being prone to going off track or losing sight of the original purpose of the task. If students periodically stop and reflect when in class, they may start to use this strategy in self-directed situations, such as when writing for homework or exams.

Over time, and as skill levels rise, it shouldn't seriously interrupt the flow of a skilled writer to think about their intended message and audience, for example, or their progress. However, as discussed in the next few tasks, some aspects of revising a text are best left until after the main composition process is complete.

Revising is Often Neglected by Students

Revising what we write is absolutely central to skilled writing, but again, beginner writers might be largely unaware of this. Children probably don't realise how much effort adults need to put into polishing a piece of writing. To an extent, they may need permission to go back and improve things. They may also incorrectly think that editing is focused only on addressing spelling and grammar (Sommers, 1980).

Research has found that revisions of a text don't happen just during redrafting. Instead, skilled authors very frequently pause to rephrase short sections of what they are writing (Bereiter & Scardamalia, 1987; Hacker et al., 2009). This fact indicates that metacognitive monitoring and control can be active during composition for skilled writers. Again, it is worth bringing this to students' attention. Otherwise, those who already do it may think that they are doing something wrong, and those who don't may not realise that it is worthwhile.

For older learners, a considerable effort can be placed on helping writers to improve the clarity and precision of their use of language. Here, writing goes hand in hand with reading (e.g. when studying what makes a written argument effective). Careful study of word meanings is also worthwhile; many older students and adults use vocabulary rather loosely. Rather than being satisfied with 'good enough' writing, we want our students to keep striving to raise their game.

Reflection and Revision

As noted earlier, revising our text as we go is a key part of skilled writing and one that needn't interrupt the flow state of mature writers. Later on, however, there comes a time to review and revise a written piece. Students may not realise that their text would benefit from redrafting (preferring to see it as 'done'), and so this is an awareness-raising task in itself.

Experienced writers have frequently noticed the benefit of a delay and of looking at a text with 'fresh eyes' (e.g. Pinker, 2015), and it may also be useful to read the text aloud to see how it sounds or use a word processor's built-in read-aloud function. As well as helping to improve the particular piece your students are working on, these are skills of planning and writing that they can take forward well beyond their school days.

By picking up slips and minor errors, these approaches help to draw attention to spelling errors and bad habits, making learners more aware of where they need to improve.

There are various more general issues that are well worth reflecting on and highlighting at the revision/redrafting stage. Often, students won't notice these things unless you draw their attention to it, and while there is no need to tackle every single one, they could be touched on periodically if they are common problems within a class. Some questions that could challenge their thinking are the following:

1. Could their piece be divided more coherently into paragraphs? (Viewing a model of a single well-structured paragraph can really help here);
2. Could some sentences be shortened for readability?
3. Could they vary the length and structure of their sentences more?
4. Could they cut down on use of the passive voice?
5. Are there precise key terms that exam markers will look for?
6. Do language choices link to the command words that exam markers focus on (e.g. using words like "therefore" when explaining or analysing a process)?
7. Does the piece have a strong start/introduction and ending?
8. Is an argument (or story) built coherently from beginning to end of the piece?

This may remind you of the powerful questions strategy (see Chapter 5); indeed, this is taking a similar approach but applied to their own work. Over time, focusing on revision of their writing helps them not just to improve but also to know what they know.

It could also be useful to draw learners' attention to the fact that detailed editing is nothing to be ashamed of. It's normal! Experienced writers edit a lot. Connected with this, it's worth noting that skilled writers *cut* a lot of text, something that school and college students may not appreciate or wish to do (Sommers, 1980). A possible way to support this skill is to aim for a higher word count for a first draft (e.g. starting at 600 words and then cutting down to 300), thus forcing them to be ruthless when coming up with a final version.

Broader Tasks

Integrating Reading and Writing

The development of reading and writing are not two separate endeavours. Far from it; better readers are better writers, and vice versa. And counterintuitively, one of the strongest, evidence-based ways to improve students' reading is for them to do more writing (Graham & Harris, 2016).

As students write, especially when their writing is in some way connected to what they have been reading, they are able to explore the ideas in ways that draw on knowledge that is fresh in their mind. It's motivating to write about something they have read about (e.g. to extend a story or respond to an argument). The reading piece also acts as a model for written style.

These points suggest a more integrated approach to reading and writing than is often taken. Rather than viewing a text such as an article or book as a resource to develop learners' reading skills, we can see it as a model for their writing and as a means of improving their metacognition about literacy more broadly. Don't neglect the potential of a good text to inspire and inform students' writing and the potential of their writing tasks to help them better understand and think more deeply about what they have been reading.

Synthesis Writing

Synthesis writing involves reading two or more texts and writing a new text:

> Synthesis writing is a type of source-based writing that requires writers to synthesize the information from different sources into a new and meaningful text. A synthesis task is a cognitively demanding, so-called hybrid task.
>
> Vandermeulen et al. (2023, p. 747)

For example, a History student may read two or more sources about an event and then write their own analysis. There are educational benefits to synthesis writing; the process of reading and rereading texts, integrating, organising, and elaborating on them causes learners to transform and engage deeply with the content (Vandermeulen et al., 2023).

In addition, there are possible metacognitive benefits. Contrasting texts (e.g. one supporting a policy and one against) helps to raise awareness that a debate exists and to reflect on their own views. Further, by seeing two or more texts in different formats, students will be prompted to think about the organisation of their own text. They will see that it needs to be similar but different, and they will have to think strategically about which aspects of the source they include and which to leave out.

Looping Reflection and Planning

Another way that literacy-based tasks can be combined more closely together may have already occurred to you from reading the earlier sections on planning and reflection. Treating these as separate tasks is missing a trick. The process of reflecting on our errors should inform subsequent tasks, and it is sensible to build on this opportunity relatively soon.

Technology might help with this. It's much easier for a teacher to model writing than reading and even better if they can share their own writing as they do it, perhaps by using a visualiser or by typing into a document that is projected onto a screen.

Literacy and Metacognition – Concluding Comments

Literacy is important to all learners – there's generally no argument about that! The core skills of reading and writing are at the heart of most English courses but also play a key role (or *could* do) in nearly every other curriculum area as well. This chapter has explored how metacognitive strategies can be applied to these situations, for literacy has certain features that lend themselves to its own set of strategies.

Where next? The past few chapters have featured many task-specific metacognitive strategies. However, there is more. As some of the examples and discussion earlier hinted at (e.g. the case of Kira's essay-writing homework in Chapter 1), metacognition doesn't just happen in teacher-led tasks. A major aspect of metacognition is what happens when a student engages in self-regulated learning. You could consider this to be *metacognition unplugged* (from teacher supervision) – situations where students must make their own choices and keep themselves motivated. Without immediate sources of support, new issues arise, and both the skills and pitfalls increase in difficulty. This will be the focus of the next two chapters.

Discussion Questions

What is the role of literacy skills in your subject?

The chapter focuses on reading and writing. Can you see links to other communication skills such as successful speaking and presentations or effective listening?

How important is writing in your classroom, and could more time be spent on tasks such as synthesis writing?

8 Metacognition Unplugged

The techniques explored so far in this book focus on classroom teaching. However, the principles apply well beyond the classroom or indeed the school. When they engage in independent work at home, in libraries, and elsewhere, many students will still misjudge how well they understand new concepts, overestimate their learning, and underestimate forgetting.

It's important for us to understand how these challenges will play out in self-regulated learning (SRL). Initially, we will focus on the bad habits and metacognitive errors that get in the way of effective studying. The reason for starting with errors and problems is simple: evidence suggests that most students are studying in flawed ways and relying on intuition rather than advice from teachers. We will therefore meet them where they currently are by thinking about the beliefs and habits that are most common.

After that, our focus will turn to the study skills that we want to see in successful self-regulated learners over the long term and to the challenges in building these skills among our students.

Self-Regulated Learning and Metacognitive Errors

What do we mean by SRL? This is learning that is done partly or entirely without supervision. It may take place in a limited sense during independent classroom tasks, both individual and group-based, including things like science practicals or sports and music practice. It also extends to projects, homework, and exam revision. The key issue is not whether the student is in school but who is making decisions about how to proceed.

The term 'self-regulation' can therefore be taken to mean any situation where a student needs to make (metacognitive) decisions about how (or when or for how long) to engage in learning or study activities rather than having a teacher direct this for them. As a concept, SRL is typically seen as broader than metacognition, as it includes emotional attributes such as students' motivation (Panadero, 2017). However, it is founded on students' metacognitive understanding of learning (Pintrich, 2002).

DOI: 10.4324/9781003386971-9

What's more, there is good evidence that metacognitive strategies are a useful focus for learners to improve. If learners focus on their own emotion, they don't get better at studying. Better strategies boost learning and can benefit emotion and motivation, too (Boekaerts & Corno, 2005). It's therefore more helpful over the long run for students to learn how to learn.

SRL is a valuable capacity for students to develop. After all, they won't be at school forever. Even in school, they may spend periods of time working on extended projects or exam revision. In such situations, the teacher can't be present to tell them exactly when they should (or should not) pre-test their knowledge, stop to look something up, persevere with a strategy or switch, or take action to improve their focus.

We have seen many examples of metacognitive errors elsewhere in this book, and these apply to independent study and self-regulated situations, too. Indeed, it's likely that the impact of metacognitive errors on students will be worse without the teacher to guide them. As an analogy, consider what a child might choose to buy from a sweet shop in comparison to a meal that their family might provide. When left to our own devices, we don't always make smart choices and do what's best for us, and that is especially true for younger learners and for those who have not yet developed an understanding of metacognition. However, we've also seen that through scaffolded support that is gradually withdrawn, students can come to have more accurate metacognition and make better decisions.

Five types of errors are worth particular attention in the context of SRL:

1. Attitudes and beliefs.
   Some students may believe that practice is pointless, that their ability is largely fixed, or even that they just "can't do" particular subjects. They may explain this in various ways; evidence suggests that biological explanations ('my brain doesn't work that way') tend to be preferred (Weisberg et al., 2008). Overall, this category includes any belief that may undermine a learner's motivation to engage in study due to the flawed notion that practice is pointless because they can't improve.
2. Goals.
   Students may think that study is valuable only as a means towards a particular end. For example, they may reason that they are learning about world history only to get an 'A', studying vocabulary in French just to pass a test, giving a talk at assembly purely to please their teacher for a reward, and so forth. Such limited, instrumental goals will also affect whether and how they engage in SRL.
3. Classification beliefs.
   Here, students label themselves as best suited to particular learning approaches (often with the enthusiastic prompting of their schools). They may be given tests that purport to provide insights into what kind of learner they are or how they should study (see Chapter 6, which outlines the 'learning styles' myth). Having internalised an inaccurate view of themselves as a learner, this may impact on later study choices. There is therefore an onus on schools to be research informed and to avoid spreading myths about how to study effectively.

4. Process beliefs.

This is where the student has a flawed idea of how information enters the memory or of the kind of strategy and process that will lead to effective learning. This includes misconceptions about how information will 'stick', such as belief that drinking more water will improve the brain's ability to take things in. It also includes a lack of awareness of processes that will hinder learning, such as failing to recognise that multitasking can be distracting.

5. Magical thinking.

This is the tendency to make wildly over-optimistic assumptions. In exercise, magical thinking might include the notion that a 1k run would cause someone to lose a few pounds in weight. When studying, it includes ideas such as that skim reading a chapter and highlighting key words constitutes learning the material or that by simply looking at a past paper and then checking the marking scheme, the student has prepared for their exam.

Task 8.1

Note down examples of the five beliefs listed in this part of the chapter. Can you think of examples that are especially relevant to your context?

If you like, you could share these examples on social media – tag me in your post!

Metacognitive errors about studying, like the ones above, are widespread – many students in your classes will exhibit at least one of these and perhaps several. It is likely that for most students, some such errors characterise the choices they make during their independent learning. And, again, the more independence that they have, the more room there is for erroneous thinking to impact on what they do.

Let's consider the following case study, which focuses on a student's self-directed study behaviours as they revise for a test (see Case Study 8).

Case Study 8:   A Chemistry Exam

Olynka is preparing for her Chemistry exam. It's one of her first major exams, and she knows that it's important. She has been studying hard.

Throughout class, Olynka has been copying from lecture slides, and she has an extensive set of notes. She also took photos of the more complicated slides, such as diagrams and graphs, that couldn't easily be noted down.

Next Olynka goes through her topics. Typically, she tackles one topic per evening in the run-up to her exam. She looks over articles and key textbook pages and highlights what she sees as the most important aspects. If she feels confused, she checks her textbook. Sometimes she reads the same section of the textbook several times and copies key quotes and ideas onto coloured index cards.

Olynka has also been diligently engaging with an online resource that provides science videos. The site shows short videos, followed by a brief test. Olynka printed out a checklist of the topics covered, and every time she gets at least 80% on one of the tests, she ticks that topic off as 'done'.

Later, a friend calls her up to speak about the exam. She tells him that she has been putting notes on coloured cards around her room because she's heard that bright colours stick in your memory better. Overall, she says, she has done a lot of work and expects to get a good grade.

After the test, Olynka gets her grade back – a disappointing 62%.

Discussion of Case Study 8

Olynka has clearly been working hard, but her approach features some of the magical thinking that often characterises students' approaches to independent learning. She is hoping for the best rather than ensuring that she knows the material thoroughly.

Olynka's approach to note-taking focuses on copying rather than summarising or using diagrams. Taking photos of diagrams is a good idea in terms of not losing key detail, but coloured notes are not automatically going to stick in long-term memory, even if they are placed prominently in her room. Olynka should instead try to actively recall her notes, making use of retrieval practice.

It's also notable that Olynka's study time happens in the run-up to exams. Covering a whole topic in one evening is too intensive and does not allow for spaced practice – another desirable difficulty (see Chapter 2). Linked to this, highlighting and re-reading are two of the least effective study methods (Dunlosky et al., 2013; see Chapter 9); her studying could be improved if self-testing were incorporated.

Olynka also relies on her subjective impressions of what she has learned. Consider how she checks her book if she feels confused and selects 'key quotes and ideas'. If her judgement is flawed here, she may not be consolidating or focusing on the right things.

It's also problematic to consider a topic 'done' after getting 80%. Having done a quiz straight after watching a video, she will have the material fresh in her mind. Her score reflects performance, not learning.

All in all, Olynka made a real effort but scored only 62%. She clearly had the commitment and desire to do better. If she had just applied a few more evidence-based practices, she could have gotten a better grade – without spending any more time on her work.

> ## Task 8.2
>
> Can you think of an example of a student who thinks and acts like Olynka from Case Study 8? Perhaps you could think of issues more directly relevant to your own sector or curriculum area. Or maybe you could think of a recent example of a student who has tackled their SRL in a notably different way from what was described in the case study. Either way, take a few minutes to jot down a vignette, describing the student (anonymising the case). This vignette could then be the focus of a group discussion with colleagues (e.g. in a staff reading group).

The Dirty Dozen of Study Habits

Another thing we can usefully learn from Case Study 8 is that certain flawed strategies are incredibly popular. Most readers of this book will have noticed students using them (perhaps you used them yourself at some point, too).

In line with what has been said in previous chapters, these flawed strategies tend to be popular because students don't have a natural or automatic insight into how learning works. Sadly, the human mind doesn't come with a user manual (Pan & Bjork, 2021). If they aren't guided, students will try to figure out studying for themselves, and they will tend to prefer flawed strategies that feel quick and easy (like highlighting) rather that desirable difficulties that are (by definition) more subjectively effortful.

Together with the misconceptions and flawed beliefs discussed earlier in this chapter, we can identify certain habits which are so widespread that they are worth commenting on one at a time. I sometimes refer to these as a 'dirty dozen' of study habits. The reason each one fails can be tied back directly to the learning and memory principles discussed in Chapter 2.

By the way, I refer to *habits* here because often these things are well practised but not carefully thought about (and because we talk about 'bad habits' in other contexts). Metacognition is all about strategy, but this implies actively thinking about your learning and making strategic choices rather than falling into a comfortable routine. Flawed study habits are often not informed by careful thinking and choices, though occasionally they may arise from genuine misconceptions. Of course, habits are not always bad, and the word 'habit' is therefore used quite loosely here, but it is useful to contrast the 12 habits below with what we might call study *skills*. The latter term implies effective strategies that have been selected by the learner for good reasons!

Habit 1: Copying Directly from Slides

There is some debate over how best to take notes (we return to this in Chapter 9) but broad agreement that meaningfully summarising notes/slides is better than copying them verbatim. When students copy, there is often very little engagement with the meaning. They could probably copy the words in reverse order without much of a loss of speed or accuracy. A meaningful summary is much preferable.

Teacher solution: The teacher or lecturer can tackle this by prompting learners to summarise and giving students time to do so and by not incentivising copying. However, it's worth noting that summarising, though an improvement on verbatim copying, is still a relatively low-impact study revision strategy (Dunlosky et al., 2013).

After moving on from a slide, you could ask a randomly picked students to give you a verbal summary of what they just took notes on. This will build in a delay, help to check that they are focusing on meaning, and send a message that just copying information is not acceptable. In addition, retrieval after a delay (even a brief delay) will be more effective than copying from a text that students can see, so a general approach of delayed summarisation can work well. Students can be advised to use the same approach at home.

Habit 2: Skim-Reading Articles

It's very tempting for learners to think that because they read something, they now know it. However, what students can do after briefly reading a text is (at best) performance, not learning.

This is not to say that skim reading is bad. Often, it's a useful, efficient strategy and a skill that every skilled reader should have. But it's important to recognise that without taking time to process the information, it won't be permanently stored in memory and will rapidly be forgotten.

Teacher solution: Learning about strategies such as skimming and scanning a text is part of a metacognitive approach to learning (see Chapter 7). The important thing is to make students realise that these each have their purpose. Skimming is very useful as a fast, efficient way of deciding which articles are relevant and which are not, for example, or finding a specific section of a long text. However, it is a very poor way of learning the information from the articles. Each skill has its own purpose.

Habit 3: Passive Re-Reading of Notes

It's not just articles and textbooks that students skim read; they do the same with their own sets of notes. Here, students probably feel a sense of familiarity with the material. They will start to experience what researchers have called an 'illusion of competence' – the sense that they know something when in fact it just feels familiar (Karpicke et al., 2009). Re-reading of notes is very passive.

Teacher solution: Beginning in the classroom and extending to self-regulated study, students need to be using their notes actively and effectively. This is exactly the sort of thing that we can teach as part of a metacognitive approach to teaching students how to learn. For example, they could be asked to transform their notes into a different format, to create a list of key points and put these onto flashcards, or to self-test by recreating the notes from memory. These strategies build in evidence-based techniques such as spacing and retrieval practice and involve actively engaging with the ideas.

Habit 4: Highlighting Notes or Handouts

Highlighting is usually not much better than passive re-reading, and like writing summaries, it is rated as a low-impact strategy (Dunlosky et al., 2013). However (again like summarising), a lot may depend on how the students go about it. The tendency of many students to cover entire paragraphs in yellow ink won't do much to get new knowledge into their minds. They may believe that it will, however, especially if they have been told that they are visual learners. Students are also more likely to re-read sections that they underlined or highlighted.

Teacher solution: Highlighting can be made more effective if it is strategic. Yue et al. (2015) found that highlighting that focuses on categorisation led to improved retention. This links to the broader principle of deep processing – thinking about the meaning of a term and how it can be categorised and linked.

Perhaps better still would be linking terms to something that is personally meaningful. Doing so leads to improved memory – a finding called the self-reference effect (Symons & Johnson, 1997). Students could be asked to highlight terms or ideas that they remember enjoying, for example, or where they can recall a specific example of having reviewed the term or written homework about it.

Another approach is to view highlighting as stage 1 of a longer process. That way, students don't need to give up their treasured highlighters but can be guided towards highlighting answers to specific questions, not everything that might be important. They could then write these questions onto flashcards, with the highlighted answers on the back. Finally, they could test themselves.

Habit 5: Saving Slideshows without Reading Them

This is like the previous habits, but worse! Many students want to have a full set of notes and will diligently file away handouts and booklets or save slideshow files to their devices. However, this is just deferring the work. They need to be encouraged to engage with the content now, not put it off.

Connected to this is the discourse about using digital tools as a second brain. These tools do, of course, have their uses, but if something is not recorded in the student's own memory, then it won't help the with understanding new material, with problem-solving, or with critical thinking (Willingham, 2008).

Teacher solution: You may wish to avoid this by not giving out handouts or files at all. However, if that isn't viable in your context, it is worth at least setting time aside to ensure that the student is engaging with the material (e.g. by verbally testing them on it after a few days).

Also, remember that handouts don't need to be exhaustive. Sometimes less is more; shorter handouts act as an aide-memoire, ensuring that nothing is missed but leaving it to students to fill in the details. (As I became more experienced as a teacher, my handouts got shorter, with more time spent exploring the material in class and more onus on students to add to written materials.)

Habit 6: Shallow Memorisation

Perhaps owing in part to the emphasis in content and grades across many educational systems, many students focus on content, mistakenly believing that they are paving the way to high achievement. Some helpful and widely recommended strategies such as quizzes and flashcards, though useful in the right context, may obscure the interconnected nature of what students need to learn. In fact, trying to memorise things without understanding them is more difficult and less effective. Expert knowledge is based on richly interconnected schemas. The more that students recognise links and hierarchies in the topic content, the more flexibly they will be able to use it and the better they will remember it.

Teacher solution: It's worth tackling this directly, perhaps with a demonstration. If you give students a list of terms to memorise without any context, these will be harder to remember than similar terms taken from a story. In general, it is worth presenting to students the ideas that memories are interconnected and that new information builds on old, just like we build up a building or collage.

On an ongoing basis, class *pop quizzes* can sometimes be followed up with penetrating questions that focus on understanding (perhaps based on *key comparisons*), both to keep students on their toes and to show that shallow memorisation is not the intended goal.

Habit 7: Commencing Study Shortly Before a Test

Evidence suggests that many students leave their test or exam preparation almost to the last minute (Kornell & Bjork, 2007). A study session the night before a big exam is almost an expectation in many contexts! However, study is much more effective if it's prolonged, as we might expect based on concepts such as the spacing effect. Although a cramming session can boost performance, the losses after that point are quite rapid because the information has not been properly contextualised and consolidated.

Teacher solution: Again, awareness raising is useful here. You might want to tackle the tendency for last-minute revision by pointing out what a waste of students' time it is to study something that will later be forgotten. Graphs such as the 'forgetting curve' could be shown on the classroom wall to further emphasise this point. (See Firth &

Riazat, 2023, for an explanation of forgetting, the forgetting curve, and the connection between meaning and memory.)

It's probably unavoidable that young people will occasionally be disorganised or demotivated, however, and we can also tackle cramming by building some study time into our classroom schedule as well. This way, any last-minute revision acts as a follow-up rather than being the only review that is done.

Habit 8: Tackling Tasks without a Moment to Reflect

As we have seen in quite a number of the tasks elsewhere in this book (e.g. *planning as the task*), taking a moment to reflect on the purpose of a task can be valuable. Even a minute at the start to reflect on what strategy to take can be worthwhile. Students often fail to do this during their SRL. Perhaps because many emphasise working hard and getting through material as fast as possible, there may be relatively little reflection on the purpose of a task. Students also appear to be quite poor at knowing when to stop – they struggle to judge where their time would best be spent, focusing on tasks of medium difficulty rather than on those skills and areas that they most need to work on (Metcalfe & Kornell, 2005).

Teacher solution: It is to be hoped that the planning and reflection strategies that you work on in class will, over time, start to transfer to students' SRL, too. However, students are creatures of habit, and without some prompting, they may well continue to study in familiar ways. For that reason, it can be worthwhile holding some study sessions in class time, running them as realistically as possible, and focusing on a small number of skills and misconceptions at a time (see also the 'Misconceptions Corner' section in Chapter 3).

Better still, you may be able to bridge the gap between such sessions and the study that students do at home by observing them when they work elsewhere in the school building – in a school library, for example. You might not want to interrupt, but rather take notes and quietly discuss your observations next time you speak to the students in class. This could lead to a teacher action research project.

Habit 9: Studying with Distractions or Music

The evidence on distractions, and especially on studying to music, is complex. What we can say with confidence is that attention is central to working memory and therefore to learning (Baddeley, 2003), and anything that interrupts or distracts learners can have an impact. This includes multi-tasking, chatting with friends alongside studying, watching TV or YouTube videos, or checking emails and messages. Phones in general can be a major distraction, drawing attention away from the task at hand.

There is also a cognitive cost of 'task switching' – even the process of stopping to engage in another task such as checking email or putting on a new music video can lead to slower and more error-prone performance in the subsequent moments (Monsell, 2003).

On the other hand, anything that students can habituate to – such as familiar music or quiet background family noise – will be less harmful (Wolf & Weiner, 1972).

Teacher solution: Work with students on this; if they are highly motivated by studying with friends, then encourage them to use this time for effective strategies like peer testing and to do tasks that require extended focus when they are alone. In terms of music, instrumental music may be less distracting than music with lyrics, at least for study tasks involving language, because lyrics disrupt the functioning of verbal working memory in a way that is fairly automatic and hard to avoid (Salamé & Baddeley, 1989).

Habit 10: Studying When Tired

Private study tends to happen after school or at weekends. Accordingly, it is not uncommon for students to tackle their homework and other tasks at times when they are tired and their attention is dwindling. This is a concern because there is a wealth of evidence that sleep plays a key role in the consolidation of new knowledge (Rasch & Born, 2013). We also know that attention is important for working memory and concentration on complex tasks (see above); again, this declines with tiredness. Although students don't always have a free choice of when to study, it's useful for them to be aware that studying when tired is less effective.

Teacher solution: Most teachers probably won't have the time and expertise to explain sleep to their students in depth, but it is worth raising at least the basics – indeed, this is probably already covered within the PSHE (personal, social, health and economic education) or wellbeing part of the curriculum. It would be worth checking that such content includes awareness raising around sleep and memory.

Bear in mind, however, that sleep is hard for young people to control, and they won't acquire better sleep habits easily, even if they are aware of the benefits. A realistic goal is to help them figure out what time of day they work best at (online 'morningness/eveningness' tests are widely used and quite helpful). You could also encourage them to cut their study sessions shorter; a brief session followed by a break and then a self-test is likely to be more effective than a longer, unbroken session in which attention starts to wane.

Habit 11: Studying in a Single Context

Students are very commonly advised to find a single quiet place to study, and there is some sense in this, given what has been said about distractions (see 'Habit 9' above). However, a lack of variation can hinder learning, and if a student is always in the same place when they engage in private study, it can make it harder for them to retrieve the information later in a new context (Smith et al., 1978) – for example, an exam hall! Likewise, it's best if they don't always try the same kind of study tasks; variation in the tasks themselves can be a desirable difficulty, as discussed in Chapter 2.

Teacher solution: As the comments above suggest, some care is needed in our advice here. If the student genuinely has only one quiet space available for independent work (e.g. a school library), then on balance they might be best to do their work there. Otherwise, it could well boost recall to study in multiple places, such as the home, library, school bus, outdoors, or in a cafe. Either way, it's worth raising students' awareness of the value of variation, something that can be built into a task. If they prefer to read and self-test, for example, they can stretch themselves by explaining the topic to a peer or writing a blog post about it. If appropriate, studying outdoors or in the school corridor could also be a form of variation.

Habit 12: Avoiding Errors

As we have seen in previous chapters, it can be beneficial to make errors during learning; this doesn't have a harmful effect and can often be beneficial to retention and understanding. Perhaps unsurprisingly, however, students don't tend to recognise the benefits of such strategies! There is a clear under-use of pre-testing or generation of their own examples among students (Metcalfe, 2017; Pan et al., 2020), and many tend to avoid the risk of errors in other contexts. For example, students may prefer to copy accurate notes rather than to self-test, even though the latter strategy is much more effective.

Teacher solution: A desire to avoid errors is closely tied to the use of effective study strategies. For example, spaced practice and varied practice are desirable difficulties and tend to lead to more errors than less effective alternatives (such as copying or re-reading). Encouraging these approaches should fit well with your metacognitive classroom, but it is worth highlighting that better strategies often lead to errors, emphasising to learners that this is not something to worry about or avoid.

Therefore, teachers may want to encourage learners to 'have a go', especially when there is a readily available method of checking and, if necessary, correcting their attempts (such as a textbook or the opportunity to submit their attempt to the teacher). It may be helpful to explain directly that errors can provide useful feedback but that avoiding errors means missing out on this opportunity and may also lead to overconfidence (Metcalfe & Finn, 2008).

Concluding Comments

In this chapter, we have begun to focus more on the learning that happens 'after the bell'. Hopefully, this chapter has indicated the size of the problem facing SRL and demonstrated that, when left to their own devices, many students won't study effectively. It is valuable for us to directly tackle these bad habits making students aware of where they are going wrong.

However, we can go further still. We don't need to be satisfied with just telling students what *not* to do. We can also model and train a programme of highly effective self-regulated studying, including the metacognitive beliefs and strategies which that entails. This is what we will turn to next.

Discussion Questions

Out of the 'dirty dozen' of study habits, which ones have you most often observed?

Are there any other bad habits related to SRL that you have noticed or problematic beliefs about learning that affect students' homework or revision?

How would you gauge the motivation of your students' SRL, and what (if anything) appears to help?

9 | Self-Regulated Study Skills

In the previous chapter, we explored some of the common beliefs and habits that students have. We saw that these can be barriers to effective learning. Often, a key priority will be to tackle misconceptions and try to break bad habits among your students.

This leads to a natural next question: what *do* we want them to be doing? The focus on the present chapter is on what highly effective study skills involve. So, what exactly does good studying look like, beyond simply avoiding the practices (such as studying with distractions) described in the previous chapter?

The good news is that much of what you have been working on in the classroom is highly relevant to self-regulated learning (SRL). Many of the strategies mentioned in Chapters 3–7 referred to providing more guidance and support early on (as a form of scaffolding) and then gradually removing this support. The goal is for your students to gain the confidence and awareness to do these things for themselves. Similar points can be seen in many of the proposed 'teacher solutions' to the bad habits discussed in Chapter 8.

There are also specific strategies which we can promote and which will be discussed in this chapter. These draw strongly on the desirable difficulties concept mentioned previously. They also follow the three phases of a task (before, during, and after) discussed earlier, though unlike with classroom tasks, the emphasis needs to be more on skills that learners can easily manage by themselves.

Desirable Difficulties

Returning to the idea of desirable difficulties and memory, it's worth noting that concepts such as retrieval practice are not study strategies per se but rather *categories*. Retrieval could be done in multiple ways! Let's consider some examples of how the five desirable difficulties outlined in Chapter 2 might play out during a student's SRL. You will notice that there is some overlap across the categories, as different difficulties often combine:

- **Challenges and active learning**: making comparisons. Asking yourself deep questions. Looking for links across and within topics. Generative tasks such as summarising, drawing diagrams, or explaining to peers. Creative tasks.

DOI: 10.4324/9781003386971-10

- **The spacing effect**: pausing mid-task and returning to it after a delay. Testing yourself after a delay. Leaving a gap between watching a video and doing review questions. Studying a topic over several days rather than all in one day/evening.

- **Embracing errors**: questioning yourself before reading a text. Trying a harder set of questions or one that you haven't looked at for a while.

- **Retrieval practice**: self-testing via quizzes or flashcards. A 'brain dump' – writing everything you can recall on a blank sheet of paper. Discussing the topic from memory or peer teaching. Summarising 'closed book', from memory.

- **Variation**: studying in many different contexts. Summarising things in several formats (e.g. orally, in writing, in a diagram). Applying concepts in several different ways. Trying different kinds of problems and tasks (e.g. multiple-choice questions, short-answer questions, essays).

Telling students how to study may not always be very motivating, as it lacks autonomy (Ryan & Deci, 2017). An alternative is to point them towards a selection of good options based on the examples above. Like a menu that has only healthy options, this could maintain a sense of control among the students while directing them towards effective choices and away from poor ones!

Lower-Impact Strategies

In their 2013 study, researchers John Dunlosky and colleagues listed ten key study strategies that are widely used by students and reviewed the evidence supporting each one. Whereas some, such as retrieval practice, were judged as 'high utility', others were ranked as medium or low (see Table 9.1). So, what is the status of these techniques? And should we recommend them?

A complexity in taking the table too literally is that the effectiveness of a strategy often depends on how it is done. How long is the spacing between two study sessions, for example? How difficult is the retrieval task?

In addition, as mentioned in the previous section, there is overlap; re-reading could be spaced out, for example, while a summary could be done from memory (thereby involving retrieval) or not. Interleaving now has more evidence behind it than was the case in 2013. We therefore shouldn't be too quick to rule out these other approaches, as some could be more or less effective depending on how they are done.

Table 9.1 The utility of study strategies based on Dunlosky et al. (2013).

High utility	Spacing; retrieval practice
Medium utility	Interleaving; Elaborative interrogation; Self-explanation
Low utility	Highlighting; Summarising, Re-reading; Imagery; Keyword technique.

What exactly are elaborative interrogation and self-explanation? Dunlosky et al. (2013, p. 6) describe elaborative interrogation as "Generating an explanation for why an explicitly-stated fact or concept is true", while self-explanation involves "Explaining how new information is related to known information, or explaining steps taken during problem solving." Broadly, both involve the student explaining information to themselves (Roediger & Pyc, 2012). These are potentially quite useful things for students to do during reading or when understanding processes in science or social science. It's also worth bearing in mind that moderate utility might be a lot better than nothing!

Meanwhile, the keyword technique is a mnemonic involved in using familiar words to help remember complex terminology. Mnemonics are helpful as scaffolding, making memories more accessible while students are still consolidating them (Firth & Riazat, 2023).

Overall, then, a focus should be on how these techniques are used. Medium- and low-utility techniques can still be part of the mix, especially if we can encourage students to combine these with spacing, retrieval, or other desirable difficulties.

Challenges with Self-Control

As mentioned in the previous chapter, effective SRL does not depend *just* on metacognition or effective study strategies. Learners also need to understand themselves, manage their own motivation, and think about the learning context (Panadero, 2017; Pintrich, 2002). We therefore need to consider a slightly broader range of evidence, such as the factors that support motivation.

Popular advice to students often encourages them to work hard or think positive (see Task 9.1). However, simply *telling* students to have a positive attitude may not be effective. It is clear from the research discussed previously in this book that students often don't know how to study and don't always know how to think about their own learning or to manage it.

In addition, while human willpower is important, attitudes and feelings don't always cause behaviour, but sometimes arise from it. For example, psychologists have described a characteristic called 'learned helplessness' where repeated failures by an animal in captivity to escape an enclosure causes them to stop trying. A similar mechanism has been suggested for human depression and apathy. In such cases, a lack of a positive attitude or will to act is the *result*, not the cause, of failure.

More broadly, our behaviours are not always the product of particular dispositions or learned traits; often, the circumstances that we find ourselves in make a major difference to how we perform. What is a student's peer group doing, for example? To stick to the analogy of healthy eating, we need to bear in mind that it is not always a case of students being 'good' or 'bad' but also whether they are in a healthy environment or social context.

Task 9.1

Take a moment to consider popular advice given to students. Examples I have seen in schools and online include 'Think win/win', 'Never procrastinate', and 'Maintain a positive mindset.' These sound like good principles – but how realistic are they? Consider how well they would work for your students. Would it be better to give them mantras that were more firmly rooted in cognitive science? Note down your thoughts, and if you like, you could try to come up with some alternative slogans.

Drawing on all of these points, and on some of the metacognitive principles explored in previous chapters, I want to explore the kind of study skills that the most successful students will engage in.

The Seven Skills of Highly Effective Students

The following list is somewhat influenced by Covey's (1989) famous 'habits of highly effective people' (for other examples, see Bin Abdulrahman et al., 2021; Eisenberg & Berkowitz, 1995). However, as noted in the previous chapter, good metacognitive practice is not something that is mainly down to habit, but rather depends on active, strategic choices (though, again, I am using both terms fairly loosely). The following therefore can be seen as the seven *skills* of highly effective students. All of these draw heavily on the ideas and research discussed in this book so far.

Study Skill 1: Understanding the Goal

Basis: Formative assessment; SRL; metacognition.

Description: It might be assumed that the first skill we consider should link to boosting memory. However, even before information can be understood and retained, it is vital that students know what they need to know (Boekaerts, 1996). The most successful self-regulated students have an awareness of what to learn and what to prioritise (Zimmerman, 2000). They ask questions to clarify a new task. They check in with teachers. When studying for formal courses, they access curriculum documents, perhaps turning them into checklists for their own use. They then transform these (e.g. by creating their own concept maps, flowcharts, and planners). And then, as learning proceeds, such students engage in formative self-testing to check their level of progress and assess what they still need to cover (Wiliam, 2011).

Study Skill 2: An Emphasis on Retrieval and Self-Testing

Basis: Retrieval practice; metacognitive monitoring.

Description: Retrieval practice is sometimes seen rather narrowly as a strategy for classroom quizzing. This can be effective, especially for encoding new factual knowledge (Agarwal & Bain, 2019; Agarwal et al., 2021), but successful students take a much broader view of retrieval. It underpins nearly every aspect of their study behaviour. Students who have mastered this skill reject passive learning techniques such as rereading, and engage actively with trying to secure things in memory via self-testing, closed book writing, and much more (Dunlosky et al., 2013). They may begin study sessions with a brain dump. They frequently and actively monitor what they know, checking to see what they can recall and whether can still recall it. If they have created concept maps (see above), they recreate these from memory. They also benefit from the formative element of self-testing and retrieval, recognising that it is hard to course-correct if you don't know what you're doing wrong. Such learners therefore engage heavily in and benefit from formative self-assessment, but they strategically use assessment as a learning strategy, too (Andrade, 2019).

Study Skill 3: Circling Back

Basis: Spiral curriculum; spacing effect; schemas.

Description: Curriculum experts have recognised for some time that learning works best as a spiral (e.g. Bruner, 1960) via which learners touch back on previous topics, linking them together with newer ideas. This way, schemas are developed. Likewise, in early childhood, the establishment of schemas is a slow but important process. Effective learners recognise that it is worth taking time to explore and understand the fundamentals of an idea rather than rushing to take in new information (Bransford et al., 2000). To add to this, the spacing effect shows us that the longer the delay between initial mastery and a review session, the more effective that review is (Cepeda et al., 2008) – something that is often overlooked by students (Koriat & Bjork, 2005). Delayed practice is best if it is combined with retrieval (see above), in what has come to be known as 'successive relearning' (Rawson & Dunlosky, 2022).

Study Skill 4: Critically Reviewing Outputs

Basis: Formative assessment; deliberate practice.

Description: Successful students are not satisfied with 'good enough'. They reflect frankly on their own progress and often actively seek out peer or teacher input into this process (Wiliam, 2011). They prefer and at times demand an honest, frank, and critical assessment of their work rather than a gentle one. Their approach is therefore less *fingers* *crossed* and more *finger on the pulse*. This formative feedback leads to self-improvement, and it is best if feedback is specific and comes from someone with sufficient expertise (Ericsson, 2017). The best students review feedback beyond what is required by a class or teacher, seeking out further insights into their progress and asking knowledgeable adults and peers for guidance.

Study Skill 5: Keeping Oneself on Track

Basis: SRL; motivation; nudge psychology

Description: Successful students keep themselves on track, managing their progress and engagement through a range of motivational tactics. However, this does not focus on reassurance or making themselves feel better. Instead, in line with the points above, the best students are critical of their own progress and are motivated by improvement. They recognise that studying sometimes gets challenging and mentally prepare for these difficult moments. They try to figure out how to improve their strategies, with a knock-on benefit to motivation (Boekaerts & Corno, 2005). They also recognise that motivation depends on a sense of competence and social connectedness (Ryan & Deci, 2017). They address these things when they are lacking, seeking out encouragement and working with peers who are similarly academically engaged. On a more day-to-day basis, successful learners use simple 'nudge' techniques such as making a public commitment or temptation bundling (combining a treat with something less pleasant, such as a study task) to keep themselves going when things get tough (Sunstein, 2014).

Study Skill 6: Managing the Flow

Basis: Flow theory; resilience; metacognitive monitoring

Description: Being in the 'flow state' is good for the quality of one's work, for level of output, and for motivation (Nakamura & Csikszentmihalyi, 2009). Successful students manage this in their work. They avoid distractions and seek tasks at the right level – a level that will challenge them but not excessively. For more difficult tasks, they have the patience to recognise that their skill will develop over time, and they tackle these only when they are ready or in small chunks. They have a degree of resilience when things are not going well, taking a break before returning to tasks, and are relatively unconcerned with others questioning the purpose or value of their studies, because their motivation is intrinsic, linked to their interest in the subject matter.

The most successful students also recognise the risks that come with the flow state, such as automatic or mindless processing, and catch themselves when this is happening. That is to say, they move their thinking to a metacognitive level spontaneously and frequently. In doing so, they get the benefit of being in flow but also of metacognitive monitoring of their work and goals.

Study Skill 7: Taking a Step Back

Basis: Metacognitive monitoring; desirable difficulties; mindset.

Description: The most successful students understand that what they are learning now is just one small part of a greater whole – their broader knowledge and skills as a human being. They are driven to be the best they can be and are patient enough to work towards it. They also reject labels that limit their potential. An element of what helps to makes them well motivated and successful is that they are not prone to popular misconceptions about learning, and they recognise that anything is possible with practice and effort. This feeds into a better attitude to learning; they exhibit a growth mindset (Dweck & Yeager, 2019) and reject the idea that some achievements or careers are beyond their ability. However, such students are also able to take a step back and reflect holistically if things are not going well. They embrace negative feedback. They can put their learning into perspective, seek help, and take tough decisions. If their learning environment is incompatible with their goals and aspirations, for example, they will seek to make a change. And just as importantly, they are aware that they may not always be correct in their views about how best to study – rather, they are suspicious when things feel too easy and are sceptical of their own assumptions (Bjork, 2018).

Task 9.2

Which of the seven study skills listed above do you consider most important? Have a go at ranking them in order in your notebook. If you had to pick one to put on your classroom wall, which would it be?

A Synthesis of Cognition and Action

You may have been surprised that the list above goes beyond the cognitive science that is the main focus of this book. It is not, for example, just a list of the best study techniques as explored by researchers like Dunlosky et al. (2013) but also includes issues around motivation and mindset.

The reason for this is that it's important to look more broadly at study behaviours and not confine ourselves just to ways that students take in new information. There are many other, broader aspects involved in how a student manages the demands of learning and improving.

However, metacognition still lies at the core. Metacognitive monitoring and metacognitive knowledge are involved in all of the strategies above in some way. Bear in mind, for example, that ideas such as seeking out feedback are based around a student's metacognitive monitoring of what they know or don't know. Their use of spacing and retrieval is based on metacognitive knowledge. All of this means that the classroom work around metacognition and self-regulation described in previous chapters can help to develop basic capacities and dispositions that will continue to be useful throughout a student's self-regulation.

As discussed earlier in this chapter, motivation and attitudes are not inherent characteristics of human beings but are influenced by the environment and by outcomes of our actions. People are more motivated towards a goal when they experience

- Minor success on the path to the goal;
- A peer group who share their goals;
- 'Nudges' that make progress towards the goal simpler and avoiding it more complex or arduous;
- A sense of identity which aligns with the goal;
- A feeling of autonomy over how to move towards the goal.

Students who are able to modify or 'hack' their own motivation to learn will be more successful, and this is part of SRL, too. It reflects a student's broader competence in knowing how to learn and knowing themselves as learners (Pintrich, 2002).

Developing Study Skills over the Long Term

One reason for scaffolding study skills is that we want to develop lifelong learners; it wouldn't be satisfactory for students to study effectively only in school, with supervision. Such individuals might fail to cope in later life.

It's worth considering that learning how to study, just as with any other skills and knowledge that students take in, is subject to a failure to transfer to new contexts (Perkins & Salomon, 1992). Even good students may struggle to apply what they have learned when the context changes.

This is all the more reason to develop study skills in an effective way. In line with what has been said about learning more generally (see Chapter 2), study skills should be learned in a way that features desirable difficulties – their practice of these skills will be spaced out over time, for example, and the context varied.

You may be working with students who have already hit upon poor study habits early in their school days, and it can be challenging for them to switch, particularly when they have previously had some academic success (Bjork & Bjork, 2023; Endres, 2023). Students may have crammed for tests and then passed those tests, for example. In this context, it can be valuable to give an evidence-based explanation of why strategies work, along with opportunities to try them (Dignath & Veenman, 2021; Yan et al., 2017). Setting specific targets to work on may also help, and peer discussions and the establishment of *metacognitive norms* can also be impactful (Endres, 2023).

Overall, it is important to recognise that learning to learn is likely to be a slow and gradual process. Starting early will be helpful, but at any stage, students can be supported in developing more effective study strategies.

Case Study 9:   A Self-regulated Student

Cammie is studying Religious Studies. They have an exam coming up, and if they pass, they will go on to university to continue their studies in both Religion and Philosophy. They are intrigued to understand the subject more deeply.

Today, Cammie is reading a text which has been carefully chosen to extend their understanding of an area of the curriculum, after discussion with their teacher. They read actively, pausing frequently and thinking about what the author is trying to say. Cammie doesn't make an active effort to memorise the text or concepts at this stage.

After a thorough initial reading, Cammie takes a tea break and thinks about the text while jotting down some notes. They create a few diagrams and concept maps to show how the text relates to others that they have read before and theories that they have studied. They also come up with their own questions regarding what else they would need to know and then message some classmates, asking for their thoughts.

Later in the day, Cammie engages in some focused self-testing, writing down everything that they can remember about what they read. They then check the original, paying attention to areas where they missed details or remembered them incorrectly. A few tricky terms and facts are identified this way, and Cammie writes these on flashcards for later review.

Time passes quickly during the self-testing phase, and Cammie recognises that they have been in a 'flow' state and lost track of time. They pause to reflect back on their initial aims before deciding that because this was an extension text, they have probably done enough for now.

Comment on Case Study 9

Cammie (see Case Study 9) sounds like a dream student! They are highly self-regulated, not only able to select appropriate study strategies but actively seeking out extra information and making sense of it. They are resilient, too, keeping themselves motivated by engaging in high-level chats with classmates.

Specific strategies that Cammie has used in the example include the following:

- Reading actively by thinking about what they want to find out;
- Self-explanation;

- Categorising and organising information;
- Retrieval practice via a brain dump and the flash cards;
- Spacing via the delayed study session and the flash cards.

All of these are worked in very naturally, and as noted earlier in this chapter, strategies can often overlap. Cammie is also very reflective. Although they have mastered the use of these strategies, their work is not automated, and they remain very aware of their progress, stopping to reflect on their aims.

Note-Taking

Note-taking can, of course, play a major role in class tasks and homework. One study that made a lot of headlines suggested that taking notes longhand was more effective than doing so via a laptop (Mueller & Oppenheimer, 2014). However, more recent research on the topic has had mixed results (e.g. Voyer et al., 2022), and overall, it seems likely that how and when the notes are taken will have a big influence.

From what has already been discussed about memory, it should perhaps be clear that taking a note of something is no guarantee that it will remain in long-term memory, particularly if nothing is done to follow up. Note-taking is better seen as a two-stage process, consisting of writing the initial notes and then reviewing and/or revising those notes. Luo et al. (2016) found that revising notes was more effective than re-copying them and also recommended the use of pauses and partners:

- A pause is where the teaching stops so that the student can take notes. This was found to be more effective than note-taking later in the day – presumably because of forgetting.
- A partner refers to discussion of notes with a partner, which was found to lead to more original notes compared to revising alone, a strategy that can be combined with a pause.

Overall, effective note-taking is an aspect of study skills, and one that may differ slightly across curriculum areas. In some cases, students could be introduced to guided note-taking formats such as 'Cornell notes', where they fill in a template rather than taking notes on blank paper.

Concluding Comments

This chapter has explored the idea of successful learners, considering what this might look like in practice. A key message is that learners need to be taught how to learn and how to study independently, in all its complexity. As we saw in the previous chapter, independent study skills don't come easy and can't be assumed. However, we can work to enhance SRL through metacognition, taking other factors such as motivation into account, too.

Having now considered both pitfalls of SRL and the fundamentals of good practice, it's time to look at some of the most extensive and demanding self-regulated tasks in education – projects.

Discussion Questions

What did you make of the suggested 'menu of healthy choices' for study strategies? Could that be applied to your curriculum area or department? What might you put on it?

How well did you feel the 'seven skills' describe the most successful students? Is there anything that you would add to these?

What is currently done to support study skills in your setting, and what more do you think should be done?

10 | Elevating Projects to the Metacognitive Level

Learning is not just about preparation from exams. Most school systems incorporate practicals and projects in some way, and students learn a lot through this practical work. In some courses, a project will be a component of the assessment – perhaps even the entire assessment. In others, they serve to consolidate other aspects of learning and to put it into more varied, realistic contexts.

Projects start early; many young children may take great pride in work that they can take home to show family members, and some devise creative projects of their own. At the upper end of the age range, school and college students may engage in fairly elaborate scholarly projects, some of which may even lead to publications (see Firth, 2019, for a discussion of students' publication of their own research).

Projects and Metacognition

As we have seen in the previous two chapters, studying independently places a particular emphasis on metacognition. This is because a student's decisions and their capacity to keep themselves on track are more impactful when the teacher is not there to prompt and guide them or to intervene when things go awry. A very similar argument holds for projects. Their nature emphasises student choices and decision-making, meaning that students' metacognitive abilities will play a part, from planning and monitoring through to the reflection phase.

Another thing that projects have in common with self-regulated learning is that they may take place mostly in the classroom, or mostly outside of it, or a mixture of the two. Other areas of a school/college could also play a part, and other people such as librarians and family members may be called upon as resources. Students need a strategic under-standing of how to manage these locations and engage with others in ways that go beyond what is needed for most independent study tasks.

It might be noted that some cognitive science researchers (e.g. Kirschner et al., 2006) have criticised discovery approaches to learning. However, the key point made in this line of research – and one which fits well with the way that the Educational Endowment Foundation present self-regulated learning – is not that discovery should never happen

DOI: 10.4324/9781003386971-11

but rather that students need sufficient expertise in order to get the most out of self-regulation. This means that learning should at first be mostly teacher-led, while the student gets to grips with new facts and skills. As things progress, tasks can become increasingly autonomous. By this point, the student knows what the issues and pitfalls are and how to utilise their own prior learning and ask the right questions.

Overall, then, project work places a strong emphasis on metacognition. To get the most from a project, it is important that students be ready for it in terms of the depth of their relevant knowledge. They will also need support with the various skills involved. These processes will be the focus of this chapter.

What is a Project, Anyway?

It can be hard to define the term 'project'. In a limited sense, any artistic output, essay, or story is a kind of project. However, for the purposes of this chapter, projects will be defined as academic tasks that include more than one distinct part and that typically require working over at least two school days and often much longer.

This means that writing a single poem or essay would not be included, even if it was completed across more than one draft. Writing and then recording a song would be seen as a project, however, as would creating a portfolio or researching and then engaging in a class debate on students' exercise habits. Any report or article which first requires conducting fieldwork or gathering data will also be seen as a project.

This definition may be narrow at times, but I will leave it to the reader's judgement whether certain briefer classroom tasks could be conceived of as projects. For example, it could be that some scenario-based tasks or extended problem-solving exercises have many of the same benefits that are discussed below:

Task 10.1

Note down two or three projects that are relevant to your context or that you have done yourself at some stage. Reflect on the idea of a schoolwork task with more than one part and completed across more than one sitting. Does this capture your notion of a project? It may be that you can think of a definition that works better in your context. If so, what are the implications for metacognition?

Projects and Learning

Projects and Prior Knowledge

It will, of course, be hard to engage in project work without the relevant knowledge. More knowledgeable learners can judge what is required and dismiss unhelpful ideas

(Tromp & Baer, 2022). Researchers call this narrowing the 'problem space'. Students' ability to do this could help teachers to judge whether the time is right for a project.

For example, if students were working on a research task, their knowledge of Mathematics and Statistics could guide their choice of what data to gather. Their understanding of research could guide them to planning methodology that is valid and ethical. The planning process would be much more efficient, with less time wasted on irrelevant ideas.

Consider some other links:

- A primary school child would tend to do a project on Ancient Egypt after learning about the topic;
- A Music student who was composing a piece would first have learned basic elements of musical theory and composition skills as well as engaging with similar musical pieces;
- A History student who was carrying out a project on a famous Victorian would need to use their understanding of the society and politics of the time in order to interpret sources.

Projects and Consolidation

Of course, projects are not just about using existing knowledge; they also stand to consolidate it. One of the best reasons for doing project work is that it applies what has been learned in a richly meaningful context. This boosts the learning of facts and skills that have previously been studied (remember – learning is not just a one-off process of putting things into memory!). As Bransford et al. (2000, p. 23) put it:

> Students' abilities to acquire organized sets of facts and skills are actually enhanced when they are connected to meaningful problem-solving activities, and when students are helped to understand why, when, and how those facts and skills are relevant.

Projects therefore have the potential to make learning come to life, in a way that is not only motivating but also important for illustrating the point of curriculum content. Projects tend to be highly memorable, and if designed well, they can make use of many desirable difficulties, such as the following:

- The spacing effect: Previously studied concepts may arise sporadically as the work is in progress.
- Retrieval: Projects feature opportunities for active recall of prior learning.
- Variation: Projects are often done in varied or unfamiliar contexts. For example, students may speak to people outside of the classroom and spend more time working in a group than is typical.

Even for proponents of more teacher-led education strategies, there is definitely a place for putting things into practice via projects if we want to achieve long-lasting learning.

Projects and Creativity

Perhaps for many educators, there is a particular kind of project that is archetypical – ones where basic skills and knowledge are applied or extended in a richer context. This kind of project is widespread and important. Such projects include things like exploring a science topic and creating a presentation based on this or carrying out multi-part data-gathering in Geography or Psychology.

However, projects can be creative too – from crafting a fiction or art portfolio to writing and recording a song, to devising a new course.

Creative projects are also extensions of prior learning. Although creativity may at times be seen as the polar opposite of memory, creativity in education depends on our knowledge, skills, and expertise. It also depends on learners' ability to plan, monitor, and reflect on their learning and benefits from effective self-regulation and therefore on metacognition. Therefore, many of the same principles discussed so far in this book apply to students' creative endeavours.

Some people may assume that creativity applies only to certain subjects (e.g. art or music), but it can play a role in any aspect of life. Indeed, projects in any subject are usually quite creative tasks because the student is creating something novel and using a method that is not entirely pre-determined. They are not simply following a set of steps provided with the teacher. This means that the project outcome will meet the standard scientific definition of creativity – making something that is new and useful (at least, new and useful to the learner).

Projects and Motivation

While there are therefore sound learning-focused reasons for project work, they are also highly motivating, at least if well designed. They are engaging and provide opportunities to explore a topic in a richly meaningful context. They also allow for a satisfying outcome that students can be proud of and (if the conditions discussed above are met) allow a sense of confidence and self-efficacy, as students realise that they have the skills to succeed. In this way, they satisfy four factors considered to be important in motivation: attention, relevance, confidence, and satisfaction ('ARCS'; Keller, 2010).

Another view of motivation, the self-determination theory of Ryan and Deci (2017), focuses on students' needs. According to this framework, people need to feel three key things in order to be motivated:

- A sense of autonomy, in that they have some choice over their actions;
- A sense of competence, feeling that something is within their capability;
- A sense of relatedness, by connecting to peers or other social groups that are important to them.

These three needs can be seen in students' hobbies and pastimes – they prefer to have a choice of what to do and tend to select activities that they are good at and that their friends also enjoy.

The same factors are relevant to projects but are not guaranteed. Projects often allow for a lot of autonomy in terms of choice of topic, though when planning tasks, teachers might want to consider how to balance freedom to choose with the need to consolidate prior learning (see above). More autonomy is motivating, but the project must be constrained enough that the work done stays relevant. For these reasons, providing a selection of choices might be more practical than total freedom.

Competence will be facilitated by putting in the right classroom preparation as discussed earlier, so that students have relevant prior knowledge and skills, allowing them to feel a sense of self-efficacy. It can also be affected by the structure of a project. A computer game is a good analogy here. Many good computer games start with simple levels or tasks that the player completes quickly and easily, but the difficulty soon ramps up. Teachers may want to design projects in a similar way.

Interactions and group work may connect to a sense of social relevance, most obviously when a project is done in a pair or group. This third factor presented by Ryan and Deci's (2017) theory – relatedness – emphasises the value of shared interests and a shared sense of ownership. It is one reason why young children enjoy showing off their work to parents. Older learners may prefer to do tasks that are respected by their peer group or seen as interesting or cool. This in turn may link back to autonomy in how topics are chosen. Overall, it's worth noting that simply putting learners into a group doesn't necessarily engage a sense of relatedness, and individual projects don't necessarily lack it.

Planning Skills and Pitfalls

The planning process, where we think about learning before engaging in the main part of a task, is a key aspect of metacognition. Chapter 4 explored the role of metacognition in setting up and planning for tasks within lessons. And as you might expect, planning is even more critical in project work. The time and thought that go in at the early stage can really pay off. As an analogy, consider how much more forethought needs to go into a multi-stage journey (e.g. to another country) compared to travelling home from work.

Planning is not a one-off process. In a similar way to the planning that happens while a student engages in extended writing (see Chapter 7), planning of a project can be returned to, developed, and refined. Any initial plan that a student makes should be seen as only a draft, open to revisions and rethinking. Ongoing reflection and re-planning will often be needed. A key metacognitive skill right from the outset is for students to be open to this process and able to recognise when the first idea is not the best.

Teachers can encourage this flexibility in planning by using more tentative language when discussing early plans in class (e.g. calling them 'initial outlines' rather than plans). It may also be helpful to set time aside to reviewing and modifying plans – the first ten minutes of the time spent on project work, for example. Asking students to reflect on what worked and what didn't go well is a useful metacognitive task in itself.

The Planning Fallacy

A psychological barrier to successful planning is a lack of awareness or prior knowledge of what the various stages of a task will involve. Fieldwork is a good example; new students of Geography or Biology may find it hard to know what to expect if they are engaging in data-gathering in the field for the first time. Even where a group has been prepared for this in class via careful briefings, the real situation will still present some surprises.

Similar challenges may be experienced in other subjects. When studying Psychology, students may have to do an ethics application process for the first time. It is easy to underestimate how long this will take or what kind of modifications might be needed to the plan.

It might occur to you that these issues would disappear over time. However, even some experience and/or information about what other students have done doesn't make planning entirely straightforward! The 'planning fallacy' is a psychological bias whereby people underestimate how long it takes to do a task. There is a wealth of evidence to show that even when provided with information that should help with accurate planning, students tend to allow far too little time (See Chapter 6).

Given how widespread the planning fallacy is, it's hard to overcome it completely. The research seems to suggest that even people with experience can fall victim to it. (You may have noticed this yourself, such as when preparing for a family event or meal or allocating time to marking!) However, there are a few things that can feature in the way we scaffold student projects:

- Set earlier deadlines than are strictly necessary, with ample time for reflection, presentation of work to peers, or similar tasks. These later stages are important and shouldn't disappear completely, but if necessary, some of this time could be borrowed for completing the core work.
- Ask students to review and modify their timeline mid-way through the project (see also the previous section). An additional benefit of this is that it may help to raise students' awareness of any failures to allow for contingencies.

It's probably natural for projects to feature a bit of hustle towards the later stages, but you may want to consider how to tap into some of that urgency a little earlier with your particular students!

Selection of Topics

Some students may simply struggle for ideas about what their project should focus on. Even those who are generally well motivated and interested in the subject might not know exactly how to transform their enthusiasm into concrete ideas. In this context, feedback will be important.

It may seem undesirable to constrain students' creativity or limit their ideas. However, research into creativity has suggested that constraints actually boost creative thinking:

> When students are asked to write a short story about anything they want, many find it difficult to get started, let alone get creative. However, when they are asked to write a story focused on a shy, red-haired boy named Colin who is missing a toe, the constraint often seems to facilitate the creative process.
>
> (Tromp & Baer, 2022, p. 1)

Some caution is needed, however. It seems likely that thinking about and working around a constraint will increase the cognitive load for students, and accordingly, their level of expertise will be relevant. For students who are complete beginners (such as the students trying out fieldwork for the first time, as mentioned above), constraints shouldn't be too limiting, as the learners don't yet have well-developed schemas that allow them to think through and overcome these limitations.

Knowing What You Know

As we have seen in previous chapters, students don't always have an accurate picture of their own knowledge. When faced with a complex project task, they may overestimate their competence or, alternatively, incorrectly believe that they know nothing of any relevance! The open format of a project, in comparison to a much more constrained classroom task such as a set of questions, can lead to a sense of panic.

A useful metacognitive approach is to make the learner's knowledge clearer to them (and you) by asking them to show what they know. A tool that's perfect for this job is a brain dump (see Chapter 9). Widely used to consolidate for retrieval practice (see Agarwal & Bain, 2019), it also helps students to reflect on what they could remember and what they struggled with.

The brain dump could be extended in various ways. One option could be to organise the ideas into a mind map or flow diagram (see "Visual Planners" section of Chapter 4). By mapping out key ideas and how these connect together, students could find it easier to locate where their main interests lie. They may also start to see connections between ideas and gaps in their knowledge that they didn't recognise before.

It is worth taking plenty of time over both the brain dump and later planning activity. Students may stop after a few minutes and say that they are finished, but new ideas (and recall of facts) can still come later in a session.

Case Study 10 shows another example of how a student engaged with a project was guided to choose and then narrow their area and later to revise their timelines.

Case Study 10:   A Psychology Project

Ramiz is studying Psychology for the first time. He needs to gather data and write a report which will account for 40% of his grade. The teacher has allocated an entire lesson for students to think about and plan their topics.

Ramiz is sure that he wants to work on human intelligence. He comes up with a plan to test the IQ of everyone in the school weekly at assembly and to track changes in their intelligence over the winter.

Through discussion, his teacher, Mrs Seal, guides him to scale back his plans, pointing out the huge practical difficulties of his initial ideal as well as ethical difficulties gathering such data from younger children.

Mrs Seal establishes that what Ramiz is really interested in is how temperature and time of year might make students more sluggish. She suggests that he look at this via a study of one class of senior pupils. They could be timed doing comparable puzzles, once in a room that is cold and again on a very sunny day when the classroom gets warmer.

Ramiz says that he will carry out the study as soon as he can and draft the report the week after, but Mrs Seal suggests that he take more time creating the research materials and allow for contingencies. She also suggests submitting drafts of his report one section at a time.

Comment on Case Study 10

The case of Ramiz demonstrates many of the issues that students may face with planning. He is hopelessly over-optimistic at first, but to his credit, he is amenable to feedback and scales back his plans.

His teacher works to figure out the real motivation behind her student's plans. When she realises that the ambition was not to gather a lot of data but to ascertain the effect of one particular factor on learning, she is able to guide him towards a more practical plan via their discussion.

Metacognition in Project Management

Now, let's think beyond the planning stage and consider various ways that metacognition plays a role throughout an extended project. This includes knowing what you know, organising information, being alert to breakthroughs, and having confidence in your own ideas. In a group project, a certain degree of managing conflicting ideas will also be important.

Building on What You Know: The Preparation Phase

Students may erroneously believe that projects are all about the 'doing'. Many want to get started straight away and fail to put into the ground work. In Case Study 10, for example, we saw a student who was hungry to get on with data-gathering. But often – especially when planning activities have indicated gaps in knowledge – the first stage of a project will involve a period of reading or other preparation that will pay dividends later.

One way to structure this phase of the project is to use the plans created earlier as a stimulus for writing questions. Peers could also help with this; classmates could look at each other's flow charts or other plans and ask clarifying questions. On the basis of this activity, students should try to list the things that they need to find out or practise ahead of the next phase of their project.

Each stage of a flow chart or branch of a mind map can lead to its own set of questions, and the questions then lead to particular targets or items on a to-do list.

Looking at examples of previously completed projects can also be helpful preparation here. These act as models for subsequent students, even when the full context is not apparent.

As mentioned in the previous section, it is useful to review and modify plans periodically. The plan should not be set in stone but rather is a first draft that can be continually improved and elaborated upon as the ideas become clearer and the knowledge and skills more secure.

Having Confidence in Your Own Ideas

A dilemma arises from the earlier discussion about modifying plans. Yes, students should be open to change and to modifying and building on earlier ideas. At the same time, most project ideas will have value if done well, and often the issue is more about scope and manageability than the idea itself. It can be rather unhelpful if a student continually doubts the value of what they are doing and feels ready to give up. At the more extreme end, some may want to restart entirely with a new idea.

Doubting the value of one's own ideas can be seen as another example of a metacognitive error. In this context, it's worth considering that motivation and curiosity are not entirely intrinsic but can build over time (O'Keefe et al., 2018). That is to say, we can *build* our passions rather than just 'discovering' them!

If motivation to persist with projects – or a desire to change track mid-way through – is proving to be an ongoing problem with your students, you might want to consider starting with a very small-scale project that has scope for expansion. That way, students gain the motivational benefits of completing the work ('satisfaction', as mentioned in the ARCS model; see above). And at that point, they can choose whether to do more with the same idea or to switch to something else entirely.

Organising Information

As students begin to gather more information and background to their project, whether this is factual information or tools and techniques, they will need a way to organise it. This will depend a lot on the student and the project, of course, and it's hard to give specific guidance. However, a few obvious possibilities include the following:

- A physical project binder or folder, kept in the classroom or schoolbag;
- An online folder that can be accessed from home or school;
- A dedicated workspace, where they can both work on and store prototypes or models.

It's also valuable to inform students about strategies or options that they might not otherwise consider, such as taking time to work in the library (not every student will have a desk or quiet space at home).

More specific issues with organisation may include note-taking and keeping track of things that they have read. As with other skills, these can be guided at first. Nobody wants to be in the situation of saying, "I read something really good about X, but now I can't find it!"

Milestones and 'Check-Ins'

As students move through a project, assuming again that this is a multi-part or multi-day task, there is no doubt that some will be making faster progress than others. In part, this is just because of individual differences, and it may also reflect varied levels of difficulty of the specific task(s) involved in the project work.

I frequently recommend that teachers avoid having one major deadline for a project to be completed in full and instead set several deadlines for milestones along the way. Depending on the project, these might include the following:

- A deadline for the project plan;
- A deadline for notes on the background research;
- A deadline for measurements or data-gathering;
- A deadline for analysis or statistics to be completed;
- A deadline for a prototype or model;
- An interim presentation to the class of their progress.

Obviously, the details will depend on the project, but the examples above will provide a starting point. Regular progress checks may add a little bit of stress or work in the short term, though most of the example listed above don't require marking, exactly, but could be checked in class. And this approach tackles the major stress and possible failure that come with a single terminal deadline.

In line with the points made earlier about the planning fallacy, periodic check-ins also provide the opportunity for a minor rethink, perhaps prompted by formative feedback from the teacher. Peer or whole-class feedback could be also be used.

It's not necessarily the case that everyone in a class will have the same deadline for these milestones. The deadlines could form part of their project plan and could depend on the nature of what they are trying to achieve. Varied or staggered deadlines could make it easier for you as teacher to feed back. In some cases, it might be helpful to schedule one-to-one chats with students, for some more individualised supervision and guidance.

Eventually, of course, there will come a point where the project has to be completed. Another worthwhile option to minimise the stress and rush that often accompany such deadlines is to have a school day that is kept completely clear to finish off any remaining aspects of the projects. This might require some negotiation with management or other colleagues, but it would have the advantage of clearing the students' schedules from other tasks, thereby allowing them the ability to focus without distractions. It would also provide the opportunity of some oversight of the final (and often crucial) last stages – perhaps with several colleagues lending a hand.

A full day allocated for project completion would also make the deadline very obvious and hard to forget for students!

Reflection

It is worth considering how and when students reflect on a project. Here, again, the accuracy of student metacognition can't be guaranteed. All the same, self-evaluation is worthwhile. In a study of older students, Frehner (2019) found that student self-evaluation of project work led to similar grades to those given by teachers and that the process engaged skills and boosted motivation. Student self-evaluation can also feed into their plans for future work. Even despite the challenges, then, there are reasons to allocate time to reflection after a project.

From the outset, it is rather more difficult to reflect on a project than it is to reflect on other kinds of tasks. A set of maths problems or even an essay, for example, will be done more rapidly, and it will be easier for students to have an overall impression of how they performed. In the case of a project, they may be reflecting on two main things, both inherently complex:

* The process undertaken;
* The project outcome.

In my experience at least, students focus strongly on the outcome and pay less attention to the process. Aspects of the process may be hard to remember, and so, when you ask them to reflect on this, it may be useful to provide some prompts, such as a reminder of earlier class sessions and activities or copies of the initial and revised plans.

Students' evaluation of project outcomes may also be biased. The nature of a project, including two or more elements, means it can be harder to judge such outcomes holistically than is the case with briefer pieces of work. The sharing of a project outcome also has an emotional impact, and students may be overly harsh in their assessment of their own work, in part because of a fear that it compares badly to others (it is, in general, easier to do a comparative judgement than a criteria-based one; Pinot de Moira et al., 2022).

The following process for student self-evaluation (adapted from Rolheiser & Ross, 2001) can be used. As will be apparent, it is most helpful if this is set into motion early, and it also ties the process of reflection into future planning, in a cycle:

Stage 1: Criteria. At this stage, students are informed of (and possibly involved in creating) the assessment criteria for the task.

Stage 2: Practice. At this stage, students are instructed in how to make accurate judgements, applying the agreed criteria to their own work. Example projects should be used for practice, and teachers can use *thinking aloud* (see Chapter 3) to make the process more explicit.

Stage 3: Feedback. Next, students are given feedback on their judgements of the practice task. The goal here is to refine their understanding of the criteria that are to be used. Peer feedback and discussion of discrepancies between classmates can be helpful here.

Stage 4: Evaluation. Now, students are ready to make judgements of their own project work, applying criteria with a fuller insight. Their judgements may still need guidance, though, and the teacher should prompt them to give full justifications: "Explain in detail why you think it meets that criterion."

Stage 5: Action plan. Finally, we come to the 'feed forward'. What lessons can be learned from the evaluation? Here, goals and an action plan can be crafted, with (ideally) some accurate metacognitive self-knowledge arising from the project work that can be usefully taken forward into future activities.

Interdisciplinary Projects

Most of the points made so far have assumed that your students will be working on a project within your subject area, but this isn't always the case. Primary practitioners in particular are often very aware that a project can draw on skills from multiple curriculum areas (e.g. science, literacy, and numeracy), though this is true for all ages. For example, students may do a project on future space travel in which they need to look at aspects of computing, wellbeing of passengers, finance, geography, the physics of launching a spacecraft, and so on.

There are many potential advantages of interdisciplinary projects. A degree of variation is built in as students come to use both/all of the subjects in new ways. For example, in connecting Maths and Psychology, students might get a more in-depth context for statistics skills and a more rigorous look at some psychological findings. The cross-curricular links may be relatively novel and exciting, too, and could link to potential careers.

Older students may need to take a more active role in setting up or exploring potential cross-curricular links. In the Scottish Baccalaureate, for example, students are expected to build on at least two of their Higher/Advance Higher subjects, and many contact researchers and interview them to find out more about cutting-edge research. In this and other more advanced and independent projects, the teacher's main role may be to check in, keep them on track (see 'periodic check-ins', above), and have some oversight of issues such as communication and research ethics.

Task 10.2

What potential is there for interdisciplinary projects in your current workplace and role? Take a moment to consider this. Perhaps you could have a coffee with one or more colleagues and brainstorm some ideas. If you do, can you think about what the benefits might be, for example, in terms of employability and transferable skills? And how would you ensure that students have the right degree of skills and knowledge so that they are ready for the project? Your thinking about these questions could be developed into a blog post about the potential and the challenges in your context.

School subjects cease to exist in higher levels of academia or in the workplace. At this point, nobody much cares which subject an idea or skill belongs to – if they need it, they learn how to do it.

What's more, many workplaces include multi-disciplinary teams. Consider a research team, for example. They may include people who are good at lab work, a project manager and/or research assistant for admin and organisation, statisticians, and also people involved in marketing or monetising the ideas developed. In education, there may be teams supporting students with additional support needs, for example.

These points are made to remind readers that the idea of a single-subject project is mainly a concern of formal academia. In the interests of developing skills that transfer to the workplace, interdisciplinary learning makes more sense. And in other situations, practising the thing you need to do is a more helpful and direct means of improvement than practising something else and hoping that transfer will somehow happen.

Concluding Comments

This chapter has shown that while projects can't always be made easier, we can analyse their features and plan for success. For example, as we have seen, this might include guiding and raising awareness of the difficulties of planning, and setting interim deadlines or check-ins. We can also be aware of the metacognitive barriers and biases that students face as they work on projects. These things all link to metacognition – to thinking about one's own thinking and learning.

Projects can really help with learning. They take us beyond the exam and have the potential for building skills that will be useful for the workplace or further study. They also (typically) feature deep, realistic problems, allowing learners to apply their knowledge in a varied and distributed way – therefore building in desirable difficulties. They can be interdisciplinary. These are all reasons that we shouldn't avoid the challenges that projects present, but think carefully about how to set students up for success and for learning.

It's now time to take a step back from specific metacognition skills and strategies and to think about how to implement a metacognitive approach to teaching in a classroom or a whole school. This will be the focus over the final two chapters of this book.

Discussion Questions

Think back to your own experience of doing projects as a child or a young adult. What went well? What problems did you experience?

What is the role of projects in your current setting?

What are your views on the potential of interdisciplinary projects or creative projects that extend or go beyond the core curriculum?

A Culture of Metacognition in the Classroom

As we have seen throughout this book so far, using better strategies isn't like learning one additional fact. It's more like levelling up what learners can do, affecting multiple future tasks. Once you know that it's helpful to stop and consider your strategy, for example, or have tools for how to plan a piece of writing, you can do it in multiple situations in the future.

By placing a focus more on *strategy* than on ability, metacognition also sends a very positive message about learning as a whole, but not an unrealistic one; we can still recognise that learners differ from each other and that, for some, academic progress will be a struggle. All the same, the idea that you can learn how to learn, and that over time a student can develop the techniques in their 'cognitive toolkit', leads to less emphasis on more fixed conceptions of ability.

Building on these ideas, this chapter explores how a teacher and their school may establish a positive learning culture and ethos. There are ways that we can foster a metacognitive culture in the classroom more generally, such that it becomes second nature for students to think about their learning, to reflect, and to use good strategies.

Cognition vs. Metacognition

To think about setting this up, it's worth briefly returning to the key idea mentioned at the outset of this book: the difference between cognition and metacognition. When a learner does something such as reading, planning, or paying attention, they are engaged in a *cognitive* process. Higher-order skills such as analysis may be more complex, but they are still cognitive processes.

A non-metacognitive approach to learning would be to emphasise automation, so that learners become better and better at doing a specific task in one particular 'right' way without stopping to think about why they are doing it that way. This is the approach to teaching and learning which I labelled 'traditional' in Chapter 1.

What makes our approach (or that of students) *metacognitive* is when the learner is more strategic or reflective about this cognition. In some way, they are thinking about

DOI: 10.4324/9781003386971-12

their thinking or about their learning – planning it, guiding it, talking about it, or reflecting on it at a later point. Metacognition is fundamental to knowing yourself as a learner and to thinking about what you know and what you don't.

A key point to make here is that this is not just about mastering a set of strategies, important as those are. It can also become an all-encompassing ethos for learning. A successful metacognitive learner is able to self-regulate their learning even away from the classroom, as discussed in Chapter 9. It has become part of their mindset. They don't let difficulties hold them back, because they know that challenges are a normal part of learning and that they can work to figure out solutions to novel problems.

If this sounds appealing, let's consider more about how to develop this as part of a broader classroom culture.

A Developing Skill

Improvements in metacognition will be gradual and cumulative, as the strategies we use interact with each other, and with other aspects of a student's thinking, learning, skills, and knowledge. We therefore need to be patient, and to look at developing metacognitive skills as a long-term project, for both ourselves and the students in our care. Researcher David Perkins (1992) described how metacognitive skills develop across four main stages (or 'levels'):

- Stage 1: Tacit. At this point, learners may have had some exposure to strategies and metacognitive language, but they are not actively using these things for themselves. They have basic metacognitive knowledge (e.g. they know that forgetting exists), but they are not fully aware of this and are not using it actively.

- Stage 2: Aware. At this level, learners show more awareness of how everyday learning tasks can be carried out with some strategic thought and intention. They understand that essays can be planned, ideas can be evaluated using evidence, and so forth. However, they don't take an active or systematic approach to using this metacognitive knowledge.

- Stage 3: Strategic. Now, we begin to talk about learners who are truly metacognitive. They make active attempts to organise their own thinking and learning. They seek out information to check the truth of an idea and try to find out which strategy would be best when tackling tasks and problems. They possess a range of strategies (at least in the subject disciplines with which they are familiar) and try to use the most appropriate one. However, these learners may still be prone to misconceptions, and their use of strategies may be rather limited in range.

- Stage 4: Reflective. At this point, learners are able to do everything that they could in the 'strategic stage'; in addition, they are adept at reflecting upon their learning. They are able to monitor the success of a strategy and change gear mid-task if necessary. If a strategy didn't work or didn't get the expected outcome, they actively try to work out why. Their deep and flexible knowledge of strategies acts as a foundation to creatively problem-solve when new strategies are needed.

The stages above should not be seen as four 'types' of learners. It's not that some people are by their nature tacit learners, for example. They are simply at an earlier stop on their journey to becoming a metacognitive learner.

However, they may stay there for quite a while – perhaps for their whole life – if we don't help to ensure that the metacognitive train leaves the station.

A Picture of Yourself as Learner

There are quite a large number of ways that students can think about, organise, or reflect on their own learning. It is generally agreed that a key aspect of metacognition is metacognitive knowledge (see also Chapter 1). This comprises what a learner knows about memory, about learning, about thinking, and so forth. It develops over time and is open to instruction (Flavell, 1979).

However, it's also important to remember that their use of strategies may be flawed. They might not make the best choice of which reading or maths strategy to use, or they may be incorrect in their view of themselves as a learner. As was mentioned in Chapter 1, it is important for learners to think more about their learning, but more important still is the accuracy of that thinking and metacognitive knowledge (Pintrich, 2002).

On this basis, the concept of metacognitive knowledge may be better viewed as metacognitive *beliefs* (Flavell, 1977; Rivers et al., 2020). These are things that students believe to be true about learning or about themselves as learners, but such beliefs are not necessarily accurate. How well we know ourselves, or the world, is always going to be a work in progress.

You might visualise this as a self-portrait. How well can you sketch yourself? Would you be able to accurately draw yourself, doing it well enough that other people can recognise you? For most people, the answer could be 'No'. Through a metacognitive approach to teaching, your students' *cognitive* self-portraits can become progressively more detailed and accurate. But they will never be perfect!

Task 11.1

Consider your own metacognitive self-portrait. Take a few minutes to jot down some observations about yourself as a learner. Next, consider how confident you are in these points. Is it possible that you are misjudging yourself? How would you know for sure?

> ## Task 11.2
>
> The idea of the metacognitive self-portrait can be adapted as a task for students to try, too. To ease them into it, begin with some simple, factual questions such as how many years they have been in school, what their favourite subject is, and when they best prefer to study. This can be followed with some deeper questions such as how they would check their own understanding or how long they would leave something before practice. Add more questions according to the age of your students and the subject(s) you are teaching!

Discourse and Beliefs

As noted above, a metacognitive approach to teaching needs to go deeper than just a set of strategies. We can't follow a recipe or blueprint. By definition, thinking has to be involved, and this is never entirely predictable.

An ethos of metacognition in the classroom therefore involves the strategies discussed earlier, and support for SRL, but there is more. There should be an overall commitment to a particular approach to learning, as we seek to set students on the journey towards more accurate beliefs about themselves. This will include the following:

- Increasing the extent to which we think about and talk about learning throughout the classroom and make active, conscious choices about how to learn;
- Expecting errors and misconceptions, tackling these along with any flawed habits that learners have picked up.

The strands above could be referred to as *discourse* and *beliefs*; you will recognise them as themes that have come up throughout this book so far. To what extent is the issue of how learning works a matter for everyday discussion in the classroom or the school as a whole? Perhaps surprisingly, the answer is 'Not much' for many schools, due to the emphasis on curriculum content. And to what extent are misconceptions about learning *actively tackled*? Without directly combatting misconceptions (e.g. via the *misconceptions corner* strategy; see Chapter 3), it's all too easy for learners to draw flawed conclusions about the outcome of their own learning.

Classroom Dialogue

This leads to issues around the general learning atmosphere and culture that you set up and foster as a teacher. Both discourse and beliefs depend heavily on what the teacher does. Discourse happens if you plan for, make time for, and model it. Consider the extent of the following in a typical lesson plan:

- Do you discuss why learners are being asked to do tasks in particular way – not just how but about why certain strategies are used within the topic?

- Do you regularly verbalise your own thinking and problem-solving (in line with *thinking aloud* and *mastering mistakes*, see Chapters 3 and 6)?

If these things are minimal or lacking entirely, a lesson plan can be a good starting point for building them in.

Expectations

Discourse can also be affected by the expectations placed on learners (e.g. when you engage in direct questioning). When the class as a whole is considered, is there an atmosphere where students are able to discuss why they think something? To give justifications? Are they expected to do so – is it the norm?

Consider, for example, a teacher who says, "Well done, Max, you got the right answer," versus one who says, "Okay, Max, thank you. Now, can you tell us why you think that's the right answer?"

The latter approach to classroom dialogue supports metacognition and also falls in line with many of the recommendations for teaching that supports communication; an example is the idea that we should promote formative assessment, support oracy, and encourage exploratory talk (e.g. Mercer, 2000; Wiliam, 2011).

However, asking an unprepared student a 'why' question may just lead to a relatively shallow response (T: "Why?"; S: "Just because!"). If deeper student responses are not currently typical among your students, it may take some practice and scaffolding to establish them. Discourse that generally encourages deep and thoughtful answers – even when these are not specifically about strategy use or learning – can pave the way for metacognitive discussions. Here are some approaches that may help to do so:

- Longer 'wait time' after questions or giving students an opportunity to jot down their thoughts on an issue or problem prior to teacher questioning;

- Modelling justifications (e.g. via written dialogues). Students could also be asked to identify language/phrases that feature justifications;

- Using paired or group discussions, with a prompt to state 'what' and 'why' for a relevant question;

- Giving pairs or small groups of students roles, with some of them in the role of prompting for reasons from their classmates (this role could rotate among the group);

- Discussing the use of these types of answers, so that students understand the value of 'why' questions on a metacognitive level.

Again, not all of these approaches are just about metacognition – thoughtful discussions could cover many issues. But it would be overoptimistic to expect such discourse to emerge by itself. As with other skills, it is worth breaking it down to basic elements, modelling these, practising them, and building a metacognitive awareness among students of what they are doing and why.

Together, over time, the discourse and dialogue in the classroom can start to build an atmosphere where reflecting on and talking about thinking or learning are seen as the norm (and, yes, this is another example of *metacognitive norms*!).

Case Study 11: German Class

Kevin is a teacher of German, working with a class who are new to the language. Today, his class have been working on the verbs for 'to be' in German.

Some of the students are struggling over the different ways to say 'you are' in German. They are finding it hard to see why there's more than one way to say this in German when there is only one way in English.

Kevin decides to tackle this via questioning. He puts it to the students that in English, there is sometimes one word that means more than one thing, and asks them to think of examples. The students suggest 'book' and 'rock' as words with more than one meaning. He then asks the students to think of cases in English where more than word can mean the same thing. Again, the students can think of several examples, such as 'nice–friendly'.

Kevin then gives pairs of students a few minutes to think about and discuss the relationship between words and their meanings, writing some prompt questions:

- Do words and meanings always match exactly?

- When we say two words mean the same thing, can there be subtle differences between them?

- If an English word can mean two different things, would you expect that to translate exactly to another language?

- Do words in German always mean exactly the same thing as words in English?

Kevin then leads a class discussion, questioning pairs about the points that they have come up with, eliciting their ideas, and scaffolding responses where necessary. During this discussion, the students' responses gradually build.

Kevin then feeds in some of the words that he found confusing when he first learned German, explaining the mistakes that he made as a new student.

To consolidate and to check that everyone understands, he asks each student to summarise the class discussion in one paragraph.

They then return to the German words.

Discussion of Case Study 11

It can be seen from Case Study 11 that Kevin used the students' confusion over German verbs to make a valuable teaching point, one that helped to correct their misconception that languages will always have a one-to-one correspondence.

It could be argued that Kevin spent quite a lot of time discussing grammar in English with his class rather than practising German. However, with a new class of learners who are tackling a language as an academic subject for the first time, it is sometimes necessary to explore and tackle misconceptions about how language learning works. These misconceptions often derive from assumptions based on prior knowledge and could cause problems later in their studies if they are not tackled. As time goes on, more and more of these discussions could happen in the target language.

Kevin also modelled his own learning process, helping to show that even teachers were beginners at one point. He gave students an opportunity to think about a problem logically and justify their thinking. In the right school culture, such dialogues could contribute to a broader capacity among students to think and argue a point.

Self-Knowledge

The approach to discourse outlined above will help to build a classroom ethos that will go beyond and extend the use of specific metacognitive strategies, seeing metacognitive talk as a norm.

This can make a real difference to supporting metacognition among a class. Even just being surrounded by discussion of how and why other learners think what they do will provide useful modelling.

Over time, as you implement the metacognitive strategies throughout this book, you can also discuss with learners what the strategies are and why they are used. This leads to what can be described as *meta-metacognition*; the learners begin to think about their own metacognition, recognising it when it happens, noticing it in others, and understanding some of its benefits.

However, this will remain implied, and certainly far from guaranteed, without direct action as part of the metacognitive classroom culture. Remember, a tacit level of metacognition is important among students but is only the beginning. Metacognitive discourse may help move learners from *tacit* to *aware*, but to fully build reflective metacognitive learners, we need to tackle beliefs more directly.

You may well hear learners saying things like:

- "Everyone learns differently";
- "My brain doesn't work that way";
- "I don't know how to study";
- "That's not how I learn".

Unfortunately, even spending some time infusing cognitive science and memory into your classroom won't entirely get rid of these naive views about learning! To develop a learning ethos that conveys the nature of learning as fluid and incremental, this has to be woven through everything that you do, so that it becomes second nature to learners. You also need to give them opportunities to discuss it, get feedback, and extend their thinking.

A major challenge here is that we require students' attitudes to change in order for behaviour to change, and the changes need to transfer to other tasks and settings as well. All of these things (attitude change, behaviour change, and transfer) are recognised by psychologists as being very difficult to achieve. Simply talking about them or hoping for the best won't do.

So, what are the best, most strongly evidence-based approaches for transforming learners' attitudes to learning within your classroom culture? We will now explore five very promising approaches. Each has its limitations and nothing is guaranteed, but it is worth noting that they can be done in combination. A many-pronged approach, if possible, could be your best bet.

Teacher Intervention

A strong message needs to come across from teachers and from schools as a whole. This means recognising that at least some of our learners will have flawed views about learning and about themselves, having confidence that we can do something about it.

Of course, this depends in part on the teacher's professional knowledge that has been discussed elsewhere in the book. One of the first things that you can do as a practitioner is to inform yourself, learning more about how memory and metacognition work (see Chapter 3), and better still if this expertise is built across the staff. The message also has to be communicated strongly. (See Chapter 12 for more about school-wide strategies and communication.)

Further, as such messages are often rather passive, the teacher needs to be directly checking on student understanding, just as you would with factual knowledge. Don't assume that it's in place (or assume the worst!). Questioning students, and doing this periodically and relatively unpredictably (but with low stakes in terms of their response), will help to embed the ideas and the high expectations that you have for them.

Direct Refutation

A further strategy that can be used to tackle flawed metacognitive self-beliefs is to directly refute some of the inaccurate and harmful beliefs that are widely held. (This is the basis of *misconception corner*; see Chapter 3.) Telling students that certain ideas are wrong is a more direct path than having them figure this out. To support a change in understanding, it may help to explain the science behind this refutation (Yan et al., 2017), doing so in an age-appropriate way.

Again, we should recognise that beliefs are hard to shift and that even when ideas have been 'debunked', students' inaccurate beliefs may linger for some time. This is another reason for tackling things more than once, returning to ideas even if you feel they have been covered, and taking the opportunity not just to consolidate their understanding but to extend and deepen it.

Particular targets for this debunking are the many neuromyths about learning that were outlined by the Organization for Economic Cooperation and Development in 2002 and have been widely researched since (e.g. Howard-Jones, 2014). These myths about the brain and learning include the following:

- The idea that not drinking enough water causes a learner's brain to shrink;
- The idea that people can be categorised according to a visual, auditory, or kinaesthetic 'learning style' (see Chapter 6);
- Variations of this above idea, such as that some people are impulsive learners and others are reflective learners (An & Carr, 2017);
- A more absolutist view that 'everyone learns in their own unique way';
- The idea that everyone is either 'left-brained' or 'right-brained';
- The idea that some people's brains can't do maths or other skills;
- The idea that only certain people can think creatively.

Arguably, these examples are just touching the surface. A range of research over decades has shown that even outside of popular myths, there is a problem in terms of how students and the general public think about memory, learning, or psychology as a whole. Myths are pervasive and widespread and are difficult to address even via training or advanced education, as evidenced (for example) by the fact that even direct refutation with teachers sometimes has short-lived benefits, with many teachers reverting to old assumptions (Ferrero et al., 2020).

This, together with the widespread endorsement of neuromyths among teachers (90%+ in some studies), may give you pause for thought. We'd like to assume that our peers are always getting things right, but many of the ideas discussed elsewhere in this book apply to educational myths too – prior knowledge (in the form of schemas) can cause distorted beliefs that are hard to overcome. Building a professional understanding of why myths are wrong is likely to help, and it won't hurt to repeat key messages frequently, via continuing professional development sessions and by sharing research and books such as this one.

Mindset

In recent years, by far the most widely discussed example of students' beliefs about learning is the concept of the growth mindset. Dweck and colleagues (e.g. Dweck & Yeager,

2019) have argued that learners need to have a general belief about the malleability of ability and about intelligence specifically:

- A fixed mindset is where learners believe that ability is fixed. They believe that either people are good at something or they are not. It doesn't change through practice. Accordingly, such learners avoid risk and prefer to do easy tasks that make them look good;

- A growth mindset is where learners believe that ability can change. They don't believe that people are inherently talented (or talentless) but rather that attainment is temporary and reflects effort and progress. Such learners embrace risk and challenge because they know that they can learn more from mistakes than from repeating easier tasks.

Perhaps unsurprisingly, Dweck and colleagues think that it's better to have a growth mindset! Strategies that might help with this include the following:

- Feedback that focuses on the task rather than the person. Not "You don't do very well at this kind of task" but "That task was clearly hard for you, but it's ok to struggle. You will get there!";

- Avoiding statements of fixed ability, even positive ones (e.g. "You're so good at this");

- Emphasising and encouraging the value of effort and learning from experience;

- Emphasising that skill and expertise are accessible to all but that gaining them is a very slow and gradual process;

- Tackling the misconception that some people are 'just naturally good at' a particular task. Often, such beliefs are overlooking the time and effort that those learners have put in.

All in all, mindset is a form of metacognition, as it involves thinking about (and beliefs about) ability and learning. It can be seen as a subset of the broader concept of thinking about thinking. As a concept and ethos, it certainly chimes well with the metacognitive discourse mentioned above.

However, some researchers have expressed scepticism about mindset-focused approaches. A key reason for this is that it's one thing to talk about mindset and another to change it! So far, efforts to make people adopt a growth mindset do appear to help, but they have rather a weak effect overall (Burnette et al., 2023). This doesn't mean we should ignore the idea of a growth mindset but does suggest that it will be very limited if we don't put other strategies in place as well.

Self-Labelling

When talking about memory and metacognition, teachers tend to focus mainly on cognition. However, emotion also has a major impact on learning. When learners say things like "I can't do science," often they are not making a logical deduction or a rational judgement but, rather, anticipating possible failure and the emotional threat that this entails.

What's more, the two interact. Who hasn't felt upset or embarrassed by a poor grade or demotivated by feeling bad at something?

As well as being inherently problematic for teachers, such self-labelling is all the more annoying because it's often inaccurate. Students label themselves incorrectly. Again, this is part of an inaccurate mental self-portrait of themselves as learners. Overall, we shouldn't shy away from emotion or the effect it has on learning. A classroom where students' basic needs are met and where they feel respected and included will be a great basis for developing a metacognitive approach to learning.

Concluding Comments

Clearly, the ways to develop metacognition and to use metacognitive strategies are the focus of this entire book. The emphasis in this chapter has been on moving away from a reliance on specific strategies (useful as those are) and towards thinking about the situation more holistically. This means an atmosphere and a culture of learning how to learn.

You may recall that one of the strategies in Chapter 3 referred to establishing *metacognitive norms*. Your job becomes much easier if students start to recognise that learning to learn is possible. The points throughout this chapter envisage a classroom where it is the norm to learn from mistakes, to question what we know, and to see learning as a skill.

Once a social norm is established, it becomes easier for students to go along with it than to deviate from this norm. A successful learning environment therefore becomes self-sustaining, less effortful for you as teacher, with the students themselves doing much of the work.

A similar argument could also be made for having a staff that learns about cognition and metacognition and where peers support each other and set high expectations. This whole-school culture of engagement with metacognition is certainly important and will be the focus of Chapter 12.

Discussion Questions

What is your response to the concept of metacognition being more than just a set of strategies?

What are your views of the 'mindset' concept, and do you think your current or recent students have shown a growth mindset?

What challenges might there be in establishing metacognitive norms in your classroom? How might you overcome some of these challenges?

12 | A Metacognition Manifesto

Throughout this book, you have learned how metacognition works, exploring its benefits and how it can be applied in practice.

We've also seen that metacognition is both a simple and a highly effective intervention, with many of its applications being 'low-hanging fruit' (see Chapter 3). It is simple in terms of being quick, cheap, and under the control of teachers. Individual practitioners working in classrooms can make more use of metacognitive strategies right away, without requiring funding, extra equipment, or a change to class sizes. There is a clear contrast with the more complex and expensive interventions that people love to talk about. And it can be very impactful as well.

However, we can't push forward with a metacognitive approach to teaching if the practitioners are not ready to engage with and, indeed, lead such an initiative.

Teachers' understanding of metacognition is the very first of the Education Endowment Foundation's seven recommendations for implementing metacognition (EEF, 2018). That makes sense – how can we implement an intervention if we don't understand it? Professional engagement was also discussed earlier in this book.

The benefits of metacognition suggest that it shouldn't be used just with your current group of students but for your whole school or college and for every learner. In this chapter, we will explore how we can work towards these aims. What does a metacognitive school or college look like? What broader approaches and values are needed in order to place an emphasis on developing independent, motivated, successful learners?

And following on from this, how can we spread the word more widely and share or model our good practice for others? What can we do to stop the message from being diluted or distorted as part of the 'lethal mutations' (Jones, 2022) that often undermine evidence-based education?

Professional Problem

Before we get into the message that can be shared, we need to consider how this message will be received. As mentioned Chapter 1, some teachers may be suspicious of metacognition as a concept, perhaps concerned that it's just the latest fad or myth.

DOI: 10.4324/9781003386971-13

Ironically, this is itself a metacognitive process. Their metacognitive beliefs about metacognition may in fact be in error!

Connected to this, the very thing that makes metacognition effective also undermines it. We have seen throughout this book that learning is challenging, that students' intuition about their progress can lead them astray, and that most people – teachers included – do not fully understand how learning works. But in line with the Dunning–Kruger effect (see Chapter 6), people don't know what they don't know. Many educators are erroneously confident about their own understanding of learning as a process.

My suggestion would be to fully embrace ideas around myths and misconceptions mentioned in Chapter 6. Debunking these and flawed recommendations that arise and are often promoted to educators is a great starting point to incite curiosity. Once people recognise that learning styles don't exist, for example, or that other popular ideas and programmes are fads based on fake science, they may be willing to at least engage in a debate and do some professional reading.

So, while studies by Howard-Jones (2014) and others have found large majorities of teachers in schools and colleges endorsing discredited ideas such as 'learning styles' or the notion that learners only use ten percent of their brains, this doesn't mean that the myths can't be overcome.

Any such engagement with the evidence is valuable. We might not agree on exactly how learning works or should be defined, but some common ground can be found in the notion that it's important – or, indeed, *necessary* – for teaching staff to have a good, professional grasp on how learning works. It's one of the things that separate us from the interested amateurs or media stars who like to comment on education. We ought to know what we are talking about when it comes to teaching and learning. And thinking about how learning works is an excellent gateway into the research on metacognition.

Balancing the Priorities

Even if the above rationale is accepted, some might still argue that a metacognitive approach to teaching is just too much for teachers to take on. Many colleagues might rightly point out that teachers already have a hard job and a lot to think about. Isn't it the case that metacognition will just add to this load? Shouldn't we instead be concentrating on core subject expertise, wellbeing, or student behaviour?

I think there are good reasons to push back against the idea that metacognition is a lower priority or should be dropped in favour of supposedly core aspects of teaching. It's true that the practitioner has a lot to think about, but that doesn't mean that teachers don't care about improving learning and outcomes. A class where the teacher has flawed subject knowledge is (of course) a huge problem, but so is one where the students are provided with accurate information but where the lesson is planned and delivered ineffectively.

I think that most teachers would agree that teaching is multifaceted. We can't focus on just one or two things, because everything that we do is interconnected. A metacognitive approach to teaching is just about taking what we are already doing and making it more effective. To ignore that is like saying that farmers should ignore fertiliser because they are too busy ploughing or that athletes are too busy in the gym to worry about nutrition. As is the case in these analogies, metacognition isn't something to do *instead of* other teaching practices. It's something that will make those practices work better.

If a teacher (particularly a new teacher) has some fundamental weaknesses in their basic teaching practice – for example, in how they ask questions or form relationships with students – then those things need to be addressed as a priority. But even then, tackling any major weaknesses we have in our practice is not something that must be done *instead* of promoting metacognitive practice. It would be best to do both.

Developing Buy-in Across the Staff

My own experience is that teachers are, by and large, rather enthusiastic to hear about the ideas presented in the early chapters of this book. Many are simply unaware of two key facts:

- The difference between learning and performance;
- The fact that student intuitions about memory often lead them astray.

Just making them aware of these issues is a great start – often, they are quick to recognise the relevance of memory to their practice, intrigued by how it is often misjudged, and enthusiastic to find out more. Most teachers also recognise some of the issues around students' failure to stay on task or overcome barriers autonomously, as tackled via strategies such as *five bees* (see Chapter 3).

However, to really be effective, the ideas have to be implemented. We've all been at in-service training workshops which were interesting, only to go back to the classroom and do everything exactly the same as before. Without a chance to put professional learning into action, simply providing information will be of limited use.

This suggests that exposure to research may helpfully raise awareness, but to make things take off, the staff really need to feel like they have some ownership. One way to do this would be to support them in running their own action research projects.

Another option would be to give different groups of staff responsibility for engaging with the research in particular areas (e.g. memory, study skills, flawed beliefs, self-regulated learning [SRL], and misconceptions) and asking them to provide regular updates to the staff as a whole. These kinds of initiatives make things feel less 'top down', as they aim to activate teachers' professional agency.

Having a colleague telling you that you've been doing everything wrong is not very motivating. It will be so much more effective to support colleagues in engaging with the evidence themselves (perhaps through books such as this one). If they do so fully and with an open mind, they may well come to similar conclusions as you have – and some will end up passionate to share the ideas more widely.

Metacognition Across Age Groups

Another obvious challenge to sharing a metacognitive approach to teaching across a whole school is the idea that some children may be too young to learn how to think strategically. One of the first major theorists of metacognition, John Flavell, was actually rather pessimistic about metacognitive functioning prior to age 7:

> young children are quite limited in their knowledge and cognition about cognitive phenomena, or in their metacognition, and do relatively little monitoring of their own memory, comprehension, and other cognitive enterprises.

> (Flavell, 1977, p. 906)

As evidence for this idea, Flavell reported on experiments that found that younger children overestimated their own readiness for a task and failed to pick up on errors in sets of instructions.

There is also neurological evidence. Metacognition depends on the functioning of the frontal lobe of the brain. This is one of the slower areas to develop, and in primary school, its interconnections with other brain areas are still very much a work in progress. Indeed, functioning in this area is still developing well into adolescence and beyond (Blakemore & Choudhury, 2006) with significant implications for teenagers' ability to engage in control and monitoring tasks.

However, we shouldn't dismiss metacognition as being too difficult, even in the early years. Children can and do talk about their own learning and forgetting from a young age. And the fact that they tend to have limited knowledge at a young age, as the Flavell quote above states, doesn't mean that we can't address this limitation.

One study by Metcalfe and Finn (2008) did so using computer-guided choices of how to learn and study with children of middle primary school age. The study found that when asked which items they should practice and re-study, children tended to make choices that were essentially random. However, when the computer guided them with choices based on theory, performance improved. This suggests that children of this age are still developing an understanding of how studying and learning work and that scaffolding will be of value – especially if the guidance is consistent with theory and evidence.

Children may also have the foundations of strategic thinking and may be able to exercise this in some contexts but not others. Thinking back to the stages discussed in the previous chapter, it wouldn't be surprising to see some younger students in the 'tacit' stage of metacognition. However, it may be the case that they behave more like 'aware' learners within their own comfort zones, such as in free play, collaborative games with classmates or family members, or when discussing stories with which they are familiar.

Overall, the approach we take can and should vary across the year groups. In that respect, it's not so different from any other area of the curriculum – adaptions need to be made for children who are both at an early stage of development and relatively

151

inexperienced. With time, their capacity to engage in the complex skills of the 'strategic' or 'reflective' stage will develop. And as with those other curriculum areas, the focus before that should be on setting the groundwork and pushing children a little bit further than their current skill level.

The requirement to think metacognitively for specific tasks will also change across the age groups. Older learners face high-stakes exams and will have to manage complex projects, alone or collaboratively. For younger students who are not yet facing external exams, the onus may be more on the teacher to guide and scaffold how they think about learning. But even very young students are engaging in independent tasks and homework.

This brings us on to questions about how the school system as a whole conceptualises and emphasises metacognition.

A Coherent Approach

Perhaps owing to the pressure for high performance in external exams and assessments, some schools place an emphasis on metacognition and (in particular) study skills from the mid-teens onwards. At this point, schools may decide to sit classes down and talk to them about how to study effectively.

However, from what we have been looking at so far in this book, you can see that metacognition as a process is too complex to grasp and embed in such a short time. If schools wait until students are in their mid-teens/in middle school, it's already too late to put the foundations in place. While advice on how to study can be useful, weaknesses in the fundamentals can't be overcome by providing a list of hints and tips in the run-up to the exams. There is a danger that such an approach is simply papering over the cracks in terms of students' broader competence as learners.

Instead, schools need to focus on building up study skills and an awareness of how learning works from the early years up. The sooner learners are guided about how to learn, the better. That way, by the time that students reach those high-stakes assessments, they are ready. They don't *need* to learn the skills of effective studying and note taking as well as their curriculum content, because they already have a strong foundation. They possess skills that can readily be adapted to a new set of challenges.

This doesn't mean that schools should be doing exam preparation from early primary school! Instead, the way we guide young people towards effective learning will differ depending on their age. This shift in emphasis may look as follows:

- Early years: Very young children are still developing, and in the early years/preschool phase, they may be mostly learning through play. All the same, children of this age have developed some awareness of their own behaviour and can talk about their own minds and those of others. Here, the emphasis should be on starting to talk to children about what is meant by learning and how decisions and memories work. They should be encouraged to reflect on decisions about how to tackle a task and to recognise that such decisions are under their control and may differ from what classmates choose to do.

- First half of primary/elementary school: At this stage, children are taking their first steps into independent study. They will be tackling their first homework tasks and reading assignments, typically doing these partly independently and partly with supervision. They may be given specific things to memorise, such as spelling lists or times tables, and so the need to understand how memory works begins in earnest.

- Second half of primary/elementary school: By now, children are carrying out homework tasks regularly and with considerably less supervision. They may engage in fairly lengthy reading activities, and as such, it's useful for them to understand the use of strategies such as self-testing and elaborative questioning. They may also have their first formal tests and exams, so understanding the role of spacing in memory is important, as is beginning to understand how to keep themselves motivated.

- Early secondary/middle school: Now, independent learning really takes off. Most children at this age can work on school-related tasks for a considerable period of time without supervision, and they can carry out lengthy multi-part projects. At the same time, education remains fairly low stakes, and so this is the perfect time to boost students' understanding of human psychology in preparation for their later studies, providing this as a topic within the curriculum to support its application to their choice of strategies. It is also valuable to point out the commonalities across different school subjects.

- Late secondary/high school: As mentioned, this is the point where many school systems have exams or other high-stakes assessments. Here, if the foundations have been put in place, students' understanding of how to learn can be refined. They should be encouraged to add to what they already know, developing a list of techniques for specific purposes, and given time to explore and discuss how these techniques link to some of the principles of human thinking and learning that they discovered earlier in their schooling. This is also an appropriate time to tackle some of the challenges involved in managing stress around exams.

- Late high school/college/university: At this point, many (perhaps most) learners have already gained some experience of doing exams or longer projects, making it the perfect time to further refine their skills and to figure out where they have been going wrong. Some may be focusing on learning discrete facts, for example, and failing to consider broader links. They will also need to tackle material and tasks with increasing levels of complexity. They should be nudged away from the idea that they can solve the challenges faced simply through reflection, perhaps by guiding them to engage with research into metacognition that explains biases and metacognitive illusions. Instead, they could look systematically and scientifically at their own learning and progress and find ways to analyse the challenges faced and to better manage time and the emotional demands of successful study.

What is presented above could be seen as the beginning of a syllabus or plan for a metacognitive approach to developing appropriate study strategies across the school years, based on teaching children about cognition and related areas of human psychology. The level of depth and detail would increase as the years go past, but a key thing to recognise is that new skills wouldn't come out of nowhere. At each point in their education, learners can be better understanding the workings of their own minds and those of other people (see Firth, 2022).

As well as fitting with children's psychological development, a coherent approach across the year groups has other another major benefit – it keeps staff on the same page and makes things less confusing for students and parents. Any curriculum aims to be sequential, both to allow coherent progression and growth and to minimise unhelpful duplication. In a very similar way, a clear plan or syllabus that covers all year groups across a whole school (or perhaps a cluster of schools, such a secondary and its feeder primary schools) would help to ensure that the offering is logical and sequential as students make their way through the school years. A similar argument could be made for the years of an undergraduate degree or other extended courses.

A more detailed, point-by-point outline of what exactly such a syllabus would look like for each age group is beyond the scope of this book, but it is worth emphasising that this could be prepared as a sequential plan, just like any other area of the curriculum. Even if you work with only one year group, you can try to get some idea of what the students can typically do at the start of the year, and build from there. But this work will be considerably more valuable if you then reach out to and communicate with colleagues who work with other ages.

The ideas discussed so far imply a certain degree of formative assessment. As with anything, there is a need to gauge progress and to recognise that different learners are at different points. As Bjork et al. (2013, p. 419) have identified: "Only rarely... are students tested for whether they have the learning skills and practices in place to take on the upcoming years of learning in an efficient, effective way." This highlights that despite the huge emphasis our schools place on testing and measurement, there is very little assessment of metacognition or study skills.

The guidance above must also take other learning factors into account and shouldn't be directly applied to all learners based purely on their age group. In any curriculum area, learners vary widely in their skills and knowledge, and any valid assessment would no doubt identify corresponding variations in metacognition and self-directed study skills.

However, a big part of a school's metacognitive approach to learning will depend on the challenges that a student is facing at a particular stage in the school system, not just their own capacities. For this reason, an overview plan like the one presented can still be useful in guiding us towards targets. Alongside this, any efforts to improve students' metacognition will be most successful if it is progressive, with foundations being well covered during the stage before.

Overall, we can't leave a metacognitive understanding of learning to chance. As a rule, learners do not tend to figure out how the mind works all by themselves, and their intuitions mislead them. What's more, the flawed strategies they use, once they have become habits, tend to stick around – most students prefer to stick in their comfort zone. It therefore makes sense to build up an understanding of learning, memory, and thinking throughout the school years.

Case Study 12: Effective Learners

Natasha is a social science teacher who has just taken on a promoted role as the Head of Teaching & Learning in her school. The school is a very large inner city secondary. It takes students from seven different primary schools, all of which are located in areas where there is significant deprivation.

Despite the challenges of the demographics, the school has a positive atmosphere and culture, with clear behaviour policies and good communication with families and support services. Students at the school are happy and well supported and have been achieving strongly in core areas. However, Natasha notices that beyond the core curriculum, they often struggle. Homework, too, is a challenge, and the students seem to lack the skills to organise their own learning. "Most of our students are not effective self-regulated learners," Natasha comments to her headteacher.

The school decide to put a plan in place to develop the self-regulation of their students. They recognise that these skills start early. This includes the metacognitive monitoring and control shown in primary school, and metacognitive knowledge of the learning process.

Natasha spends time in the feeder primary schools. In some, she notices that while students are doing well in areas like literacy and maths, this is based on quite a traditional approach to pedagogy, based heavily on repetition. The students are capable and confident in the areas that they have covered recently but inflexible and prone to forgetting. They also struggle to transfer what they have learned to new contexts – something that will be important when applying literacy and numeracy across the curriculum in secondary school. However, other primary schools place a strong emphasis on metacognition, encouraging children to become owners of their own learning.

Natasha convenes a series of meetings and a conference with the main contacts in the primary schools. She invites experts from outside of the schools, including psychologists and researchers. Primary colleagues are encouraged to share best practice, while Natasha and fellow secondary practitioners team give insights into the challenges and expectations faced by students when they reach the secondary stage. Staff also hear from some current secondary school students, who reflect on their educational journey from primary to secondary school.

Through these meetings, working collaboratively, Natasha and the other professionals start to formulate a plan for supporting metacognition and SRL through different years of the school system.

Comment on Case Study 12

The practice described in the case study is mixed in terms of its effectiveness, and this is likely to be the case across many clusters of schools. Some schools favour a traditional approach to teaching (see Chapter 1), as this has helped them to ensure high attainment in 'the basics'. However, when Natasha and colleagues in partner schools take a step back, they can see that this is of little avail if the students can't use what they have learned flexibly in future.

It is, of course, unfortunate that many of Natasha's students have got to secondary school and are still, despite their various achievements and the positive ethos of the school, ineffective learners overall. However, on the positive side, this is not the case for all. Natasha has recognised that there is some excellent practice taking place in the feeder primaries, and she is taking steps to help this be shared more widely.

It's good that they are hearing from students, too, though, of course, there is a need to be cautious about how to use this feedback, given that even successful students' reflections are not always accurate (see Chapter 6).

Overall, the case study shows two main things. Firstly, developing metacognition and self-regulation benefits from a collaborative approach, with efforts to make things work as a system, and across different year groups. Secondly, even with external support, this is not going to be a quick fix. After various meetings and a conference, Natasha and colleagues are only starting down the road of applying a metacognitive approach across their school network.

A Manifesto

So far in this chapter, we have considered the role of teachers' professional understanding and of the development that students make in their metacognition across their years of education. These macro-level considerations point towards a general framework, within which all of the skills and strategies of this book can sit.

They also imply the need to communicate such an approach more broadly. It is a great thing for one teacher to be engaging in excellent metacognitive-based practice but is so much more powerful if the whole staff are doing so. What you do will have a stronger effect if all teachers in the school/college (or most people, at least) are pulling in the same direction. What's more, this will directly affect the skills and ethos of the students who come through your classroom door next year.

The rest of this chapter focuses on a specific blueprint for how 'learning to learn' can be implemented by schools as a whole. The approach taken in the following list of points assumes that you have at least *some* influence over what goes on at a wider level than your own classroom. I will suppose, for the purpose of the following points, that you are part of a team or working group with responsibility to advise your school on how to support metacognition and effective study throughout your centre.

If you are engaging with this as an individual and haven't yet formed a larger community, I hope that you will nevertheless see the value in a shared message and 'manifesto' for a metacognitive approach to teaching. Even if you have no direct leadership role or general responsibility for teaching and learning in your context, you can still help to spread the message and, in doing so, be at the cutting edge of educational changes that will reach your setting sooner or later. You may even come to be regarded as an expert who can advise others on the best approaches to use.

And if you are a school leader, you are in a perfect position to take the following ideas and implement them straight away.

Ten Priorities

The following section draws on what has been said so far by presenting ten key priorities for implementing metacognition across a school. These are listed in three sub-sections, titled *Challenge our Thinking*, *Build the Foundations*, and *Fine-Tuning*. As a group, they make up the manifesto referenced in the chapter's title – a programme for implementing and perfecting a metacognitive approach to teaching on a whole-school level.

Challenge Our Thinking

Priority 1: Embrace a Metacognitive Approach to Teaching

It might sound obvious, but our very first priority must be to embrace this approach to teaching as a whole, as discussed at the start of this chapter. Doing so indicates a willingness not only to try out the strategies described in this and other books about metacognition but to adopt them systematically. It means not dipping our toes into the water of cognitive science, or using only a few selective strategies, but diving right in.

Along with this, embracing the approach means embracing the metacognitive approach to teaching outlined in Chapter 1, and supporting learner flexibility and deep thinking. This is the approach of schools that value having their students understand why they are learning, and developing the ability to transfer ideas learned in school to new, unpredictable contexts.

As a policy, this priority aims to develop learners who don't just have knowledge and skills (although those are, of course, important) but who are also strategic and self-regulating. And it avoids lip service or 'tick box' approaches to metacognition or to cognitive science more broadly.

In short: we need to commit to this!

Priority 2: Acknowledge the Problem

Regardless of how on board with the cognitive science agenda your current school or college might be, your next priority should be to recognise that there is a problem. Indeed, we need to shout about this fact, getting the message out loud and clear: metacognition is hard, and can't be left to take care of itself.

Acknowledging the problem means that schools need to recognise the counterintuitive nature of learning and the fact that performance doesn't indicate learning. This can't be repeated often enough! We are still swimming against the current – a current set in motion by decades of educational tradition. We need to be saying, "No – getting the answers right by the end of class is not enough."

The second aspect of 'the problem' is that metacognition takes time. As we have seen from the preceding sections of this chapter, and from case study 12, metacognition is not something that can be left to the last minute or built up rapidly through a one-off workshop or an intensive study skills session. Nor does it make sense to support student metacognition via brief or one-off actions, as most would quickly forget what they have been told. Studying effectively is a skill, just like a sport or playing a musical instrument, and can't be developed overnight. It certainly shouldn't be left until the final years of school.

In short: we need to recognise that this won't be easy.

Priority 3: A Multifaceted Concept

As well as being challenging to establish, metacognition is a complex phenomenon. The skill of effective learning is in fact a set of skills, capacities, and dispositions. There's not just one aspect of metacognition, and therefore we can't say to teachers, "Just do this, and everything will be fine". There is no blueprint that will work in every context. Likewise, even a skilled and committed teacher who has embraced the problems outlined above can't assume that because they are using a set of metacognitive tasks and strategies, the job is done.

A further challenge is when metacognition is seen as synonymous with study skills (or, worse, with exam skills). Schools should recognise that metacognition encompasses a wide range of situations, including both teacher-led and SRL tasks. Nor is boosting exam attainment the only goal of establishing a metacognitive approach to teaching. It can also impact, for example, on students' creativity, wellbeing, workplace-relevant skills, and lifelong learning. However, some fellow teachers may not understand this and may assume that this is mainly or only about boosting students' ability to revise for exams and/or their grades. It is a broad skill of how to learn that should prepare students for situations in school and beyond.

We therefore need to challenge our thinking. Any time we feel that we have 'got' metacognition, we should try to further widen the scope of what should be covered.

In short: think bigger!

Build the Foundations

Priority 4: Engage Staff with Research

A vital step towards school improvement is for the staff to inform themselves and to keep informing themselves and staying up to date with research.

Implementing a metacognitive approach to teaching depends upon the teachers' own knowledge and understanding. We can hardly expect students to take the kind of aware, strategic, and reflective approach described in previous chapters if we don't understand it ourselves. As has been argued with respect to SRL: "teachers themselves need a firm intellectual understanding of the... construct" (Boekaerts & Corno, 2005, p. 222).

In short: Hit the books!

Priority 5: Draw on Existing Expertise

No school or college is starting from scratch; each institution already has a staff of diversely talented teachers. A great principle for any school-wide development would be to draw upon and develop this existing staff expertise (a good example of this is shown in Case Study 12).

What's more, simply imposing a new plan on staff could cause some bad feeling. Instead, schools can involve teachers in the planning process, identify where there are particular pockets of expertise, and encourage the establishment of professional learning communities with time and resources. Teacher action research can be supported, too.

More broadly, networks of practitioners can be encouraged across different schools and via school–university partnerships. Some may already exist.

In short: Don't neglect staff expertise.

Priority 6: Build a Coherent Syllabus

As discussed earlier in this chapter, there is a risk that well-intentioned attempts to build metacognitive competence in learners are poorly followed up as students move from year to year. There could be changing priorities and inconsistent terminology or messages.

By analogy, imagine that everyone just tried to teach some maths but without a coherent curriculum to guide the endeavour overall. It's easy to see how things could get confusing, and benefits could be hit or miss.

Now, it's surely the case that some support for metacognition is better than nothing. Better still, though, would be a coherent, school-wide metacognitive syllabus. This will aim to build metacognition and SRL across the different year groups, accounting for age and development. At its core will be a coherent plan for new skills that will be developed across each school year and also a common vocabulary. However, there will also be sufficient scope for personalisation by teachers and according to subject, as well as plenty of chances to return to extend metacognitive learning over different years, via a spiral curriculum. The outline shared earlier in this chapter can make for a good starting point.

In short: Have a plan!

Priority 7: Tackle Myths and Misconceptions

Many flawed ideas about learning and memory may seem like common sense at first glance, and as mentioned earlier in this chapter, neuromyths are widely endorsed by teachers internationally. It is entirely possible for teachers to be on board with cognitive science and metacognition, and even to be evidence-engaged more broadly, yet still believe some of these myths. The best approach, therefore, is to tackle them directly, with a challenge and 'debunking' communicated strongly and repeatedly at a whole-school level.

As well as outright myths, there may be lingering misconceptions about a range of learning-related ideas, such as mistaking engagement for learning; the concept of learning vs. performance (see also priority 1); or the idea that creativity applies only to certain subjects. The 'learning pyramid' is another flawed idea, endorsed by many teachers. Schools might expand on the *misconceptions corner* technique, sharing this across the whole school, discussing the flawed educational idea in staff meetings, and targeting it in communications with students and parents.

In short: Tackle myths head on.

Fine-Tuning

Priority 8: Be Sensitive to Different Contexts

As schools get more of a handle on a metacognitive approach to teaching, certain difficulties will arise along the way. The precise use of strategies may differ across different curriculum areas or across primary and secondary. It's necessary to avoid over-simplistic messages about what metacognition involves.

Metacognition and SRL may also look different depending on the learning situation and task, taking into account the demands and skills involved. SRL of project work, for example, has particular demands that differ from those of many classroom exercises, and these complexities interact with differences across the year groups. The idea of a menu of study strategies (see Chapter 9), for example, will work best at the departmental level. The same menu couldn't serve every age group and curriculum area.

This priority, therefore, advocates for a contextualised approach to metacognition. Typically, the best person to decide on the specific metacognitive priorities for a particular group of students will be the classroom teacher, with support from their department – but this depends on their professional knowledge (see priority 4 above).

In short: Make space for nuances.

Priority 9: Make It Visible

It's one thing to say that something is a priority in some kind of school plan document. It's another to make it obvious to each and every person who walks into the building.

Take a look around your workplace and ask yourself what students and visitors will see. Are there any visible indications that the school cares about metacognition? Or does it seem that the priorities lie elsewhere?

One immediately visible way for schools to share this as a priority will be to display information around metacognition and study skills in the school. Terms and definitions could be prominent on noticeboards. Case studies of learners talking about their study skills could be presented as posters (the case studies from this book could also be adapted), while graphics used around the school corridors or in parental newsletters could act as very salient reminders about the issues.

In short: Use visible reminders.

Priority 10: Get Off to a Good Start

As explained earlier, the skills and knowledge involved in learning effectively can't be developed overnight. An effective school-wide approach to metacognition recognises that implementation will take time and that it will benefit from a coherent syllabus across the year groups. But what does this look like right from the start?

Because of the tendency to focus on the advanced study skills needed to tackle high-stakes exams, it is easy to neglect the foundations. And these foundations – which include a basic understanding of memory, learning, and how one's own mind works, as a willingness to learn more – should be laid carefully with learners at a young age.

Accordingly, it is important to get students off to a good start, building the foundations for effective and thoughtful approaches to learning so that there is no need to cram for exams or paper over the cracks at a later point.

Children who are just starting primary/elementary school may be too young to have a sophisticated control over their own learning, but it's important that they be asked to think about what school is for and continually hear messages that emphasise the importance of interest and curiosity, and metaphors for learning as a skill like any other.

In short: don't neglect the first years of school.

Priority 11: Reach Out to Parents

Parents are just as susceptible to myths and misconceptions about learning. Some may give well-meaning advice to young people, such as "Study hard", unaware that successful learning is more about strategy than about desire. This puts the onus on schools to guide and advise parents and carers on study skills and SRL.

To avoid parents giving messages that detract from the metacognitive approach that a school is embracing, it will be valuable to work with parents and help them to understand this approach. This could happen through in-person sessions, emails, and other communications or a combination of these things.

Such communications could compare learning to other skills, using metaphors such as learning art or learning to drive to help parents understand the importance of time, practice, and feedback. Targets that form part of a school's plans should be repeated frequently with examples, and myths should be tackled head-on as they would be with teachers. Finally, parents should be advised that students' intuitions about learning are unreliable. Rather than ask their young people "How confident are you about topic X?", the teacher could say "Tell me what you know about topic X" (in line with the *prove it* strategy).

In short: engage and align with parents.

Prority 12: Harness Motivation

It's valuable to avoid being too prescriptive in terms of how students work in class or how classes are planned, as many teachers chafe against such micromanagement (Skinner et al., 2021). Students, too, may reject metacognitive strategies if these don't align with their priorities or support a sense of autonomy (Ryan & Deci, 2017).

This means that any strategy to promote metacognition needs to be implemented carefully and with motivation in mind. A school-wide approach to metacognition is by its nature top-down, and this means being even more careful.

In short: Stay mindful of people's wants and needs.

Concluding Comments

In this chapter, we have seen that metacognition can be best applied in an integrated way across the school system, not just in individual classrooms. A coherent approach will consider developing skills and competence gradually, introducing children to fundamental concepts in an age-appropriate way and then building on this in future years. It will also respectfully consider the role of parents and differences across curriculum areas.

I hope you now feel informed and inspired, ready to implement a metacognitive approach to teaching in your classroom and beyond!

Discussion Questions

What challenges would you face in implementing a metacognitive approach to teaching on a whole-school basis?

What are the key areas of professional expertise in your setting?

What professional contacts do you have that could help?

References

Agarwal, P. K., & Bain, P. M. (2019). *Powerful teaching: Unleash the science of learning*. John Wiley & Sons.

Agarwal, P. K., D'Antonio, L., Roediger, H. L., McDermott, K. B., & McDaniel, M. A. (2014). Classroom-based programs of retrieval practice reduce middle school and high school students' test anxiety. *Journal of Applied Research in Memory and Cognition, 3*(3), 131–139.

Agarwal, P. K., Nunes, L. D., & Blunt, J. R. (2021). Retrieval practice consistently benefits student learning: A systematic review of applied research in schools and classrooms. *Educational Psychology Review, 33*(4), 1409–1453.

An, D., & Carr, M. (2017). Learning styles theory fails to explain learning and achievement: Recommendations for alternative approaches. *Personality and Individual Differences, 116*, 410–416.

Anderson, R. C. (2018). Role of the reader's schema in comprehension, learning, and memory. In D. E. Alvermann, N. J. Unrau, M. Sailors, & R. B. Ruddell (Eds.) *Theoretical models and processes of literacy* (7th ed., pp. 136–145). Routledge.

Andrade, H. L. (2019). A critical review of research on student self-assessment. *Frontiers in Education, 4*, 87.

Atkinson, R. C., & Shiffrin, R. M. (1968). Human memory: A proposed system and its control processes. In K. W. Spence & J. T. Spence (Eds.), *The psychology of learning and motivation* (Vol. 2, pp. 89–195). Academic Press.

Ausubel, D. P. (1968). *Educational psychology: A cognitive view*. Holt, Rinehart & Winston.

Avargil, S., Lavi, R., & Dori, Y. J. (2018). Students' metacognition and metacognitive strategies in science education. In Sjöström, J., Eilks, I., Dori, Y. J., Mevarech, Z. R., & Baker, D. R. (Eds.), *Cognition, metacognition, and culture in STEM education: Learning, teaching and assessment* (pp. 33–64). Springer.

Baddeley, A. (2003). Working memory: Looking back and looking forward. *Nature Reviews Neuroscience, 4*(10), 829–839.

Bartlett, F. C. (1932). *Remembering: A study in experimental and social psychology*. Cambridge University Press.

Bauernschmidt, A. (2017). Guest post: Two examples are better than one. *Learning Scientists Blog*. https://www.learningscientists.org/blog/2017/5/30-1

Bereiter, C., & Scardamalia, M. (1987). *The psychology of written composition*. Lawrence Erlbaum.

Bin Abdulrahman, K. A., Khalaf, A. M., Bin Abbas, F. B., & Alanazi, O. T. (2021). Study habits of highly effective medical students. *Advances in Medical Education and Practice, 12*, 627–633.

Bjork, E. L., & Bjork, R. A. (2011). Making things hard on yourself, but in a good way: Creating desirable difficulties to enhance learning. In Gernsbacher, M. A., Pew, R. W., Hough, L. M. & Pomeranz, J. R. (Eds.), *Psychology and the real world: Essays illustrating fundamental contributions to society* (pp. 56–64). Worth.

Bjork, R. A. (2018). Being suspicious of the sense of ease and undeterred by the sense of difficulty: Looking back at Schmidt and Bjork (1992). *Perspectives on Psychological Science, 13*(2), 146–148.

Bjork, R. A., & Bjork, E. L. (2023). Introducing desirable difficulties into practice and instruction: Obstacles and opportunities. In Overson, C. E., Hakala, C. M., Kordonowy, L. L., & Benassi, V. A. (Eds.), *In their own words: What scholars and teachers want you to know about why and how to apply the science of learning in your academic setting* (pp. 19–30). Society for the Teaching of Psychology.

Bjork, R. A., Dunlosky, J., & Kornell, N. (2013). Self-regulated learning: Beliefs, techniques, and illusions. *Annual Review of Psychology, 64*, 417–444.

Blakemore, S. J., & Choudhury, S. (2006). Development of the adolescent brain: Implications for executive function and social cognition. *Journal of Child Psychology and Psychiatry, 47*(3–4), 296–312.

Boekaerts, M. (1996). Self-regulated learning at the junction of cognition and motivation. *European Psychologist, 1*(2), 100–112.

Boekaerts, M., & Corno, L. (2005). Self-regulation in the classroom: A perspective on assessment and intervention. *Applied Psychology, 54*(2), 199–231.

Bransford, J. D., Brown, A. L., & Cocking, R. R. (2000). *How people learn: Brain, mind, experience and school.* National Academy Press.

Bruner, J. S. (1960). *The process of education.* Harvard University Press.

Bryce, T. G. K., & Blown, E. J. (2023). Ausubel's meaningful learning re-visited. *Current Psychology.*

Burnette, J. L., Billingsley, J., Banks, G. C., Knouse, L. E., Hoyt, C. L., Pollack, J. M., & Simon, S. (2023). A systematic review and meta-analysis of growth mindset interventions: For whom, how, and why might such interventions work? *Psychological Bulletin, 149*(3–4), 174–205.

Carvalho, P. F., & Goldstone, R. L. (2014). Putting category learning in order: Category structure and temporal arrangement affect the benefit of interleaved over blocked study. *Memory & Cognition, 42*(3), 481–495.

Cepeda, N. J., Vul, E., Rohrer, D., Wixted, J. T., & Pashler, H. (2008). Spacing effects in learning a temporal ridgeline of optimal retention. *Psychological Science, 19*(11), 1095–1102.

Cialdini, R. B., Wissler, R. L., & Schwietzer, N. J. (2002). Science of influence. *Dispute Resolution Magazine, 9*, 20–22.

Covey, S. (1989). *The 7 habits of highly effective people.* Free Press.

Dent, A., & Koenka, A. C. (2016). The relation between self-regulated learning and academic achievement across childhood and adolescence: A meta-analysis. *Educational Psychology Review, 28*, 425–474.

Deuja, A., Kohn, N. W., Paulus, P. B., & Korde, R. M. (2014). Taking a broad perspective before brainstorming. *Group Dynamics: Theory, Research, and Practice, 18*(3), 222–236.

Dignath, C., & Büttner, G. (2008). Components of fostering self-regulated learning among students. A meta-analysis on intervention studies at primary and secondary school level. *Metacognition and Learning, 3*, 231–264.

Dignath, C., & Veenman, M. V. (2021). The role of direct strategy instruction and indirect activation of self-regulated learning: Evidence from classroom observation studies. *Educational Psychology Review, 33*(2), 489–533.

Dirkx, K. J. H., Camp, G., Kester, L., & Kirschner, P. A. (2019). Do secondary school students make use of effective study strategies when they study on their own? *Applied Cognitive Psychology, 33*, 952–957.

Dunlosky, J., Rawson, K. A., Marsh, E. J., Nathan, M. J., & Willingham, D. T. (2013). Improving students' learning with effective learning techniques: Promising directions from cognitive and educational psychology. *Psychological Science in the Public Interest, 14*, 4–58.

Dweck, C. S., & Yeager, D. S. (2019). Mindsets: A view from two eras. *Perspectives on Psychological Science, 14*(3), 481–496.

Education Endowment Foundation (EEF). (2018). *Metacognition and self-regulated learning: Guidance report. EEF Website*. https://educationendowmentfoundation.org.uk/public/files/Presentations/Publications/Metacognition/EEF_Metacognition_and_self-regulated_learning.pdf

Ehrlinger, J., Johnson, K., Banner, M., Dunning, D., & Kruger, J. (2008). Why the unskilled are unaware: Further explorations of (absent) self-insight among the incompetent. *Organizational Behavior and Human Decision Processes, 105*(1), 98–121.

Eisenberg, M. B., & Berkowitz, R. E. (1995). The six study habits of highly effective students: Using the big six to link parents, students, and homework. *School Library Journal, 41*(8), 22–25.

Endres, T. (2023). Adaptive blended learning to foster self-regulated learning: A principle-based explanation of a self-regulated learning training. In Overson, C. E., Hakala, C. M., Kordonowy, L. L., & Benassi, V. A. (Eds.), *In their own words: What scholars and teachers want you to know about why and how to apply the science of learning in your academic setting* (pp. 378–394). Society for the Teaching of Psychology.

Ericsson, K. A. (2017). Expertise and individual differences: The search for the structure and acquisition of experts' superior performance. *WIREs Cognitive Science, 8*(1–2), e1382.

Ferrero, M., Hardwicke, T. E., Konstantinidis, E., & Vadillo, M. A. (2020). The effectiveness of refutation texts to correct misconceptions among educators. *Journal of Experimental Psychology: Applied, 26*(3), 411–421.

Ferrero, M., Vadillo, M. A., & León, S. P. (2021). A valid evaluation of the theory of multiple intelligences is not yet possible: Problems of methodological quality for intervention studies. *Intelligence, 88*, 101566.

Festinger, L. (1954). A theory of social comparison processes. *Human Relations, 7*(2), 117–140.

Firth, J. (2018). Is it all just memorisation? *The Profession: The Annual Publication for Early Career Teachers, 1*, 31–35.

Firth, J. (2019). *The teacher's guide to research: Engaging with, applying and conducting research in the classroom*. Routledge.

Firth, J. (2021). Boosting learning by changing the order and timing of classroom tasks: Implications for professional practice. *Journal of Education for Teaching, 47*(1), 32–46.

Firth, J. (2022). Understanding the human mind – a foundation for self-regulated study. *Impact, 14*, 6–9.

Firth, J. (2023). Interleaving. In Jones, K. (Ed.), *The researchED guide to cognitive science* (pp. 55–68). John Catt.

Firth, J., & Riazat, N. (2023). *What teachers need to know about memory*. SAGE.

Flavell, J. H. (1971). First discussant's comments: What is memory development the development of? *Human Development, 14*(4), 272–278.

Flavell, J. H. (1977). *Cognitive development*. Prentice-Hall.

Flavell, J. H. (1979). Metacognition and cognitive monitoring: A new area of cognitive–developmental inquiry. *American Psychologist, 34*(10), 906–911.

Frehner, M. (2019). Self-and peer-evaluation of individual project work: An innovative course assessment method to increase student motivation. In S. Mukherjee (Ed.), *Teaching methodologies in structural geology and tectonics* (pp. 5–41). Springer.

Gathercole, S. E. (2008). Working memory in the classroom. *Psychologist, 21*(5), 382–385.

Gattegno, C. (1963). *Teaching foreign languages in schools: The silent way*. Educational Explorers.

Gick, M. L., & Holyoak, K. J. (1983). Schema induction and analogical transfer. *Cognitive Psychology, 15*, 1–38.

Graham, S., & Harris, K. R. (2016). A path to better writing: Evidence-based practices in the classroom. *The Reading Teacher, 69*(4), 359–365.

Gube, M., & Lajoie, S. (2020). Adaptive expertise and creative thinking: A synthetic review and implications for practice. *Thinking Skills and Creativity, 35*, 100630.

Hacker, D. J., Keener, M. C., & Kircher, J. C. (2009). Writing is applied metacognition. In D. J. Hacker, J. Dunlosky, & A. Graesser (Eds.), *Handbook of metacognition in education* (pp. 154–172). Routledge.

Halamish, V. (2018). Pre-service and in-service teachers' metacognitive knowledge of learning strategies. *Frontiers in Psychology, 9*, 2152.

Hatano, G. & Inagaki, K. (1986). Two courses of expertise. In H. Stevenson, H. Azuma & K. Hakuta (Eds.), *Child development and education in Japan* (pp. 262–272). Freeman.

Hattie, J., & Clarke, S. (2018). *Visible learning: Feedback*. Routledge.

Hattie, J. A., Biggs, J., & Purdie, N. (1996). Effects of learning skills interventions on student learning: A meta-analysis. *Review of Educational Research, 66*(2), 99–136.

Henrich, J., Heine, S. J., & Norenzayan, A. (2010). The weirdest people in the world?. *Behavioral and Brain Sciences, 33*(2–3), 61–83.

Hirsch, E. D. (2003). Reading comprehension requires knowledge of words and the world. *American Educator, 27*(1), 10–13.

Hogarth, R. M., Lejarraga, T., & Soyer, E. (2015). The two settings of kind and wicked learning environments. *Current Directions in Psychological Science, 24*(5), 379–385.

Howard-Jones, P. A. (2014). Neuroscience and education: Myths and messages. *Nature Reviews Neuroscience, 15*(12), 817–824.

Jones, K. (2022). *Lethal mutations in education and how to prevent them*. https://evidencebased.education/lethal-mutations-in-education-and-how-to-prevent-them/

Kang, S. H. K., Pashler, H., Cepeda, N. J., Rohrer, D., Carpenter, S. K., & Mozer, M. C. (2011). Does incorrect guessing impair fact learning? *Journal of Educational Psychology, 103*(1), 48–59.

Karpicke, J. D., Butler, A. C., & Roediger III, H. L. (2009). Metacognitive strategies in student learning: Do students practise retrieval when they study on their own?. *Memory, 17*(4), 471–479.

Keller, J. M. (2010). *Motivational design for learning and performance: The ARCS model approach*. Springer.

Kellogg, R. T. (2008). Training writing skills: A cognitive developmental perspective. *Journal of Writing Research, 1*(1), 1–26.

Kirschner, P. A., Sweller, J., & Clark, R. E. (2006). Why minimal guidance during instruction does not work: An analysis of the failure of constructivist, discovery, problem-based, experiential, and inquiry-based teaching. *Educational Psychologist, 41*(2), 75–86.

Koriat, A., & Bjork, R. A. (2005). Illusions of competence in monitoring one's knowledge during study. *Journal of Experimental Psychology: Learning, Memory, and Cognition, 31*(2), 187–194.

Kornell, N., & Bjork, R. A. (2007). The promise and perils of self-regulated study. *Psychonomic Bulletin & Review, 14*(2), 219–224.

Kornell, N., & Bjork, R. A. (2008). Learning concepts and categories: Is spacing the "enemy of induction"? *Psychological Science, 19*, 585–592.

Krashen, S. D., & Terrell, T. D. (1998). *The natural approach: Language acquisition in the classroom*. Prentice Hall.

Lemov, D. (2019). *Tracking the data: From classroom to soccer pitch*. https://teachlikeachampion.org/blog/tracking-the-data-from-classroom-to-soccer-pitch/

León, S. P., Panadero, E., & García-Martínez, I. (2023). How accurate are our students? A meta-analytic systematic review on self-assessment scoring accuracy. *Educational Psychology Review, 35*(4), 106.

Luo, L., Kiewra, K. A., & Samuelson, L. (2016). Revising lecture notes: How revision, pauses, and partners affect note taking and achievement. *Instructional Science, 44*, 45–67.

Marsh, E. J., & Roediger, H. L. (2013). Episodic and autobiographical memory. In A. F. Healy & R. W. Proctor (Eds.) *Handbook of psychology, Vol 4: Experimental psychology* (pp. 472–494). Wiley.

McCabe, J. A. (2018). What learning strategies do academic support centers recommend to undergraduates?. *Journal of applied research in memory and cognition, 7*(1), 143–153.

Mercer, N. (2000). *Words and minds: How we use language to think together.* Routledge.

Mestre, J. P. (1994). Cognitive aspects of learning and teaching science. In S. J. Fitzsimmons & L. C. Kerpelman (Eds.), *Teacher enhancement for elementary and secondary Science and Mathematics: Status, issues, and problems*; NSF 94-80 (pp. 31–53). National Science Foundation.

Metcalfe, J. (2017). Learning from errors. *Annual Review of Psychology, 68*, 465–489.

Metcalfe, J., & Finn, B. (2008). Evidence that judgments of learning are causally related to study choice. *Psychonomic Bulletin & Review, 15*, 174–179.

Metcalfe, J., & Kornell, N. (2005). A region of proximal learning model of study time allocation. *Journal of Memory and Language, 52*, 463–477.

Miller, G. A. (1962). *Psychology: The science of mental life.* Harper & Row.

Moll, L. C., & Gonzalez, N. (1994). Lessons from research with language-minority children. *Journal of Reading Behavior, 26*(4), 439–456.

Monsell, S. (2003). Task switching. *Trends in Cognitive Sciences, 7*(3), 134–140.

Mueller, P. A., & Oppenheimer, D. M. (2014). The pen is mightier than the keyboard: Advantages of longhand over laptop note taking. *Psychological Science, 25*(6), 1159–1168.

Muijs, D., & Bokhove, C. (2020). *Metacognition and self-regulation: Evidence review. Education Endowment Foundation.* https://bep.education/wp-content/uploads/2020/05/Metacognition_and_self-regulation_review.pdf

Nakamura, J., & Csikszentmihalyi, M. (2009). Flow theory and research. In C. R. Snyder & S. J. Lopez (Eds.), *Handbook of positive psychology* (pp. 195–206). Oxford University Press.

Neisser, U., & Harsch, N. (1992). Phantom flashbulbs: False recollections of hearing the news about Challenger. *Affect and Accuracy in Recall: Studies of "Flashbulb" Memories, 4*, 9–31.

Nelson, T. O. (1996). Consciousness and metacognition. *American Psychologist, 51*(2), 102–116.

Nelson, T. O., & Narens, L. (1990). Metamemory: A theoretical framework and new findings. *Psychology of Learning and Motivation, 26*, 125–141.

Newcomb, N. S. (2023). Constructing a canon for the science of learning. In Overson, C. E., Hakala, C. M., Kordonowy, L. L., & Benassi, V. A. (Eds.), *In their own words: What scholars and teachers want you to know about why and how to apply the science of learning in your academic setting* (pp. 8–18). Society for the Teaching of Psychology.

O'Keefe, P. A., Dweck, C. S., & Walton, G. M. (2018). Implicit theories of interest: Finding your passion or developing it?. *Psychological Science, 29*(10), 1653–1664.

Pan, S. C., & Bjork, R. A. (2021). Acquiring an accurate mental model of learning: Towards an owner's manual. In A. Wagner & M. Kahana (Eds.), *Oxford handbook of learning & memory: Foundations and applications.* Oxford University Press.

Pan, S. C., Sana, F., Samani, J., Cooke, J., & Kim, J. A. (2020). Learning from errors: Students' and instructors' practices, attitudes, and beliefs. *Memory, 28*(9), 1105–1122. https://doi.org/10.1080/09658211.2020.1815790

Panadero, E. (2017). A review of self-regulated learning: Six models and four directions for research. *Frontiers in Psychology, 8*, 422.

Pashler, H., McDaniel, M., Rohrer, D., & Bjork, R. (2008). Learning styles: Concepts and evidence. *Psychological Science in the Public Interest, 9*(3), 105–119.

Perkins, D. N. (1992). *Smart schools: Better thinking and learning for every child.* Free Press.

Perkins, D. N., & Salomon, G. (1992). The science and art of transfer. In A. Costa, J. Bellanca & R. Fogarty (Eds.), *If minds matter: A foreword to the future, 1* (pp. 201–210). Skylight.

Pinker, S. (2015). *The sense of style: The thinking person's guide to writing in the 21st Century.* Penguin Books.

Pinot de Moira, A., Wheadon, C., & Christodoulou, D. (2022). The classification accuracy and consistency of comparative judgement of writing compared to rubric-based teacher assessment. *Research in Education, 113*(1), 25–40.

Pintrich, P. (2002). The role of metacognitive knowledge in learning, teaching, and assessing. *Theory into Practice, 41*(4), 219–225.

Rasch, B. & Born, J. (2013). About sleep's role in memory. *Physiological Reviews, 93*(2), 681–766.

Rawson, K. A., & Dunlosky, J. (2011). Optimizing schedules of retrieval practice for durable and efficient learning: How much is enough?. *Journal of Experimental Psychology: General, 140*(3), 283–302.

Rawson, K. A., & Dunlosky, J. (2022). Successive relearning: An underexplored but potent technique for obtaining and maintaining knowledge. *Current Directions in Psychological Science, 31*(4), 362–368.

Reynolds, K. J., Subašić, E., & Tindall, K. (2015). The problem of behaviour change: From social norms to an ingroup focus. *Social and Personality Psychology Compass, 9*(1), 1–12.

Richland, L. E., Kornell, N., & Kao, L. S. (2009). The pretesting effect: Do unsuccessful retrieval attempts enhance learning?. *Journal of Experimental Psychology: Applied, 15*(3), 243–257.

Rivers, M. L., Dunlosky, J., & Persky, A. M. (2020). Measuring metacognitive knowledge, monitoring, and control in the pharmacy classroom and experiential settings. *American Journal of Pharmaceutical Education, 84*(5), 7730.

Robertson, B. (2021). *The teaching delusion 2: Teaching strikes back.* John Catt.

Roediger, H. L., & Karpicke, J. D. (2006). Test-enhanced learning: Taking memory tests improves long-term retention. *Psychological Science, 17*, 249–255.

Roediger, H. L., & Pyc, M. A. (2012). Inexpensive techniques to improve education: Applying cognitive psychology to enhance educational practice. *Journal of Applied Research in Memory and Cognition, 1*(4), 242–248.

Rolheiser, C., & Ross, J. A. (2001). Student self-evaluation: What research says and what practice shows. In R. D. Small, & A. Thomas (Eds.), *Plain talk about kids* (pp. 43–57). Center for Development and Learning.

Ryan, R. M., & Deci, E. L. (2017). *Self-determination theory: Basic psychological needs in motivation, development, and wellness.* Guilford Publications.

Salamé, P., & Baddeley, A. (1989). Effects of background music on phonological short-term memory. *Quarterly Journal of Experimental Psychology, 41*(1), 107–122.

Salomon, G., & Globerson, T. (1989). When teams do not function the way they ought to. *International Journal of Educational Research, 13*(1), 89–99.

Sanna, L. J., & Schwarz, N. (2007). Metacognitive experiences and hindsight bias: It's not just the thought (content) that counts!. *Social Cognition, 25*(1), 185–202.

Sawyer, R. K., & DeZutter, S. (2009). Distributed creativity: How collective creations emerge from collaboration. *Psychology of Aesthetics, Creativity, and the Arts, 3*(2), 81–92.

Shore, R., Ray, J., & Gooklasian, P. (2015). Applying cognitive science principles to improve retention of science vocabulary. *Learning Environments Research, 18*, 233–248.

Singer Trakhman, L. M., Alexander, P. A., & Sun, Y. (2023). The effects of processing multimodal texts in print and digitally on comprehension and calibration. *Journal of Experimental Education, 91*(4), 599–620.

Skinner, B., Leavey, G., & Rothi, D. (2021). Managerialism and teacher professional identity: Impact on well-being among teachers in the UK. *Educational Review, 73*(1), 1–16.

Slavin, R. E. (2013). Effective programmes in reading and mathematics: Lessons from the best evidence encyclopaedia. *School Effectiveness and School Improvement, 24*(4), 383–391.

Smith, S. M., Glenberg, A., & Bjork, R. A. (1978). Environmental context and human memory. *Memory & Cognition, 6*(4), 342–353.

Soderstrom, N. C., & Bjork, R. A. (2015). Learning versus performance: An integrative review. *Perspectives on Psychological Science, 10*(2), 176–199.

Sommers, N. (1980). Revision strategies of student writers and experienced adult writers. *College Composition & Communication, 31*(4), 378–388.

Sunstein, C. R. (2014). Nudging: A very short guide. *Journal of Consumer Policy, 37*, 583–588.

Sweller, J., Ayres, P. L., Kalyuga, S. & Chandler, P. A. (2003). The expertise reversal effect. *Educational Psychologist, 38*(1), 23–31.

Symons, C. S., & Johnson, B. T. (1997). The self-reference effect in memory: A meta-analysis. *Psychological Bulletin, 121*(3), 371–394.

Terry, D. J., & Hogg, M. A. (1996). Group norms and the attitude-behavior relationship: A role for group identification. *Personality and Social Psychology Bulletin, 22*(8), 776–793.

Tromp, C., & Baer, J. (2022). Creativity from constraints: Theory and applications to education. *Thinking Skills and Creativity, 46*, 101184.

Tversky, A., & Kahneman, D. (1974). Judgment under uncertainty: Heuristics and biases. *Science, 185*(4157), 1124–1131.

van der Zee, T., Davis, D., Saab, N., Giesbers, B., Ginn, J., van der Sluis, F., Paas, F, & Admiraal, W. (2018, March). Evaluating retrieval practice in a MOOC: How writing and reading summaries of videos affects student learning. In *Proceedings of the 8th international conference on learning analytics and knowledge* (pp. 216–225).

Vandermeulen, N., Van Steendam, E., & Rijlaarsdam, G. (2023). Introduction to the special issue on synthesis tasks: Where reading and writing meet. *Reading and Writing, 36*, 747–768.

Veenman, M. V. J., Van Hout-Wolters, B. H. A. M., & Afflerbach, P. (2006). Metacognition and learning: Conceptual and methodological considerations. *Metacognition and Learning, 1*, 3–14.

Voyer, D., Ronis, S. T., & Byers, N. (2022). The effect of notetaking method on academic performance: A systematic review and meta-analysis. *Contemporary Educational Psychology, 68*, 102025.

Wasik, B. A., Hindman, A. H., & Snell, E. K. (2016). Book reading and vocabulary development: A systematic review. *Early Childhood Research Quarterly, 37*, 39–57.

Weisberg, D. S., Keil, F. C., Goodstein, J., Rawson, E., & Gray, J. R. (2008). The seductive allure of neuroscience explanations. *Journal of Cognitive Neuroscience, 20*(3), 470–477.

Wells, G., & Loftus, E. F. (2013). Eyewitness memory for people and events. In R. K. Otto (Ed.) *Handbook of psychology, Vol 11: Forensic Psychology* (pp. 617–630). Wiley.

Wiliam, D. (2011). *Embedded formative assessment.* Solution Tree Press.

Will, K. K., Masad, A., Vlach, H. A., & Kendeou, P. (2019). The effects of refutation texts on generating explanations. *Learning and Individual Differences, 69*, 108–115.

Willingham, D. T. (2008). Critical thinking: Why is it so hard to teach?. *Arts Education Policy Review, 109*(4), 21–32.

Wolf, R. H., & Weiner, F. F. (1972). Effects of four noise conditions on arithmetic performance. *Perceptual and Motor Skills, 35*(3), 928–930.

Wong, S. S. H., & Lim, S. W. H. (2022). Deliberate errors promote meaningful learning. *Journal of Educational Psychology, 114*(8), 1817–1831.

Yan, V. X., Soderstrom, N. C., Seneviratna, G. S., Bjork, E. L., & Bjork, R. A. (2017). How should exemplars be sequenced in inductive learning? Empirical evidence versus learners' opinions. *Journal of Experimental Psychology: Applied, 23*(4), 403–416.

Yue, C. L., Storm, B. C., Kornell, N., & Bjork, E. L. (2015). Highlighting and its relation to distributed study and students' metacognitive beliefs. *Educational Psychology Review, 27*, 69–78.

Zimmerman, B. J. (2000). Self-efficacy: An essential motive to learn. *Contemporary Educational Psychology, 25*, 82–91.

Index

Page numbers in *italics* refer to figures, page numbers in **bold** refer to tables, and page numbers in ***bold italics*** indicate a reader task.

Printed in the United States
by Baker & Taylor Publisher Services

Printed in the United States
by Baker & Taylor Publisher Services